MW00512317

Stu Spike

BREAKING THE TREASURE CODE

THE HUNT FOR ISRAEL'S OIL

by

James R. Spillman

&

Steven M. Spillman

True Potential Publishing

Travelers Rest, South Carolina

Published by:
True Potential Publishing
PO Box 904
Travelers Rest, SC 29690
info@tppress.com
www.tppress.com

Scripture quotations in this volume are from the King James Version of the Bible unless specifically credited to another source.

Scripture quotations noted (NASB) are from the New American Standard Bible, copyright © 1960, 1962, 1968, 1971, 1972, 1973, 1975, 1977 Lockman Foundation (used by permission)

Scripture quotations noted (NIV) are from the New International Version copyright © 1973, 1978, 1984 International Bible Society. Used by permission of Zondervan Bible Publisher

THE TREASURES OF THE DEEP is reprinted with permission of Lion's Lamb Publications, Lucerne Valley, CA

THE GREAT TREASURE HUNT
Original copyright 1981, Omega Publications
P.O. Box 4130, Medford, OR 97501

ISBN 0-9767811-0-7

Library of Congress Control Number: 2005905158

Printed in the United States of America

Dedication

To the memory of James R. Spillman, who walked with God and served Him in life. The evidence of his labor on earth continues today to bear fruit in the lives of those he touched.

"Being confident of this very thing, that he which hath begun a good work in you will perform it until the day of Jesus Christ:" Philippians 1:6

Acknowledgements

John Brown of Zion Oil & Gas Company for his continued faith and dedication to the fulfillment of the promise of oil in Israel.

> *Also concerning the foreigner who is not of thy people Israel, when he comes from a far country for Thy name's sake (for they will hear of Thy great name and Thy mighty hand, and of Thine outstretched arm); when he comes and prays toward this house, hear Thou in heaven Thy dwelling place, and do according to all for which the foreigner calls to Thee, in order that all the peoples of the earth may know Thy name, to fear Thee, as do Thy people Israel, and that they may know that this house which I have built is called by Thy name.*
>
> *I Kings 8: 41 – 43*

Gene Soltero, Philip Mandelker, Stephen Pierce, Stacy Cude and Glen Perry of Zion Oil & Gas Company for their time and instruction in their individual fields of expertise.

Jerry McGlothlin of SpecialGuests.com for his advice and brilliant title suggestion.

Theologian Dr. Roger Luther for his study and analysis of related scriptures.

Always to my wife, friend and partner, Elaine. Every venture is a joint venture.

CONTENTS

BOOK I

AN ETERNAL COVENANT FOR THE ISRAEL OF GOD
Riches Underground

FROM OLIVE OIL TO PETROLEUM
From Titusville to Opecville • Prayer, Blood, and
Oil • Later Oil Discoveries • Hidden Riches

JACOB: THE BEGINNING
Jacob Adopts Two Sons • Why Would Jacob
Adopt His Grandsons? • Jacob's Last Blessing

THE HEAD OF JOSEPH
Keeping Joseph in Sight • Following the Sons
•Joseph Left a Heritage • Recapping the Clues •
Consider the Rosetta Stone

ISRAEL, THE LAND
From Egypt to the Jordan • The Song of Moses •
The Inheritance of the Nations • When was This
Inheritance Given? • Jacob is the Center •

Sucking Oil! • Moses' Blessing • Between His Shoulders? • Joseph's Head Returns • The Blessings of the Other Brothers • *"Blessings of the Deep that Lieth Under"* • Another Hebrew Parallelism • Joseph is Represented by His Two Sons • *"Rejoice in Thy Going Out"* • Gad of the Torn Arm • Asher Dips His Foot in Oil • The Fountain of Jacob • Is Joseph's Well an Oil Well?

BREAKING THE CODE

We find Joseph's Head • The Profile of Joseph's Head • Joseph's Shoulders • Gad's Torn Arm • Asher Dips His Foot in Oil!

A "P.S." ON JACOB'S BLESSINGS

"The Fatness of the Earth" • Let's Recap • When Will This Oil Be Found?

GOG AND MAGOG

The Hooks in the Jaws • It is Only a Matter of Time • The Last Days • What is the Timetable? • The Wastes Shall Be Builded • *"Thou Shalt Think an Evil Thought"* • The World Sees God's Holiness

WHAT ABOUT ARMAGEDDON?

Power Blocs of the Nations • The Revived Roman Empire • The Kings of the South and East • The Whole Earth is Against Zion! • Christ's Triumphant Return

BOOK II

SIGNIFICANCE

Ishmael, Isaac, Jacob, & Esau • Perspective •
The Lesson • God's Purpose • Prophecy Fulfilled
• The End of Days • Gog and Magog • The End
Game

APPENDICES

SPIRITUAL HELP

ZION OIL & GAS VISION BOOK

Introduction

Stories of buried treasure have fascinated people for thousands of years. Discovering an ancient map; digging through clues hidden in a forgotten manuscript; piecing together the fragments of a mysterious puzzle; until eureka! The answer is revealed! The location of a lost treasure; hidden for ages, until now! The clues, the map, the reasons, the ancient stories, all the puzzle pieces fit together. X marks the spot. You have located a treasure that has been buried for ages!

Alas! Beware! Buried treasure often holds a purpose of its own. Hidden long, long ago by its owner, it was to be uncovered later when circumstances were ripe for its use. The treasure's first owner, its true owner, had his own purpose in mind when he buried the treasure here. But it's been discovered now, ages later, by you. You are the new owner and you now have claim to the treasure. As your property it will serve your purpose...or will it? Are you really its rightful owner? Perhaps ownership has never really changed hands? Perhaps the treasure was meant by its original owner to lay hidden until the time you, or someone like you, uncovered it? Perhaps this was the original owner's intent. Perhaps now, ages later, the treasure has been uncovered to serve its first owner's purpose. But what purpose could its first owner possibly mean for the treasure to serve today?

The Hunt Begins

This book is the story of a treasure hunt; possibly the most important treasure hunt in our history. Not just because of the size of the treasure; but because of the implications of its discovery. When this treasure comes to the surface the world will change. Its unearthing may herald the end of this age of man and the beginning of a new age.

Many steps of the treasure hunt have already been completed. The clues have been revealed. The X has been located. The hole has been dug. The treasure has been sighted. The part of the story yet to be told is what will happen when the treasure is brought to the surface. Will it bring wealth and blessing to those who find it? Will it bring a curse? What will the neighbors think? Whose purpose will the treasure serve? Does it have a purpose of its own; maybe that of its original owner? Discovering the treasure is one thing, what happens when it comes to the surface will be another thing entirely!

Our treasure story begins at the kitchen table of a cookie-cutter home, in a neighborhood of cookie-cutter homes in Southern California. The year is 1973. A grocer and a preacher sit at the table.[1] Spread out before them are paper cut-outs. A map of the land of Israel, cut into puzzle pieces. They are in the shape of the twelve ancient tribal territories of Israel; territories delineated more than three thousand years ago. A Bible lays open, in front of the grocer. A pad, filled with scribbled notes is at his right hand. He is explaining the puzzle, excitement rising in his voice as he moves pieces into place, flipping the pages of his Bible to obscure passages in the books of Genesis and Deuteronomy. The preacher listens, first politely with just a hint skepticism; then with mounting interest, as the grocer unfolds his story and the map pieces come together. The scriptures at first seem vague and unrelated, but together they build to make

---

[1] Jim Gerard (the grocer) and Jim Spillman

the grocer's case. Unbelievably, the map confirms the scripture clues - head, crown, foot, and arm! *"This is something. This is really something!"* thinks the preacher. Finishing his explanation the grocer glances up, searching for some reaction in the preacher's eyes or in the expression on his face. The preacher shakes his head in amazement of what has just been revealed. *"Jim"*, he says to the grocer, *"we'd better pray about this"*. They bow their heads over the map pieces, notes and the open Bible spread out in front of them. The clues have been revealed. The treasure hunt has begun.

The Book

My father, Jim Spillman, wrote a book in 1981. It was a small paperback; just 79 pages. It wasn't his first book, certainly not considered his most significant; just a little paperback. The book was titled, ***"The Great Treasure Hunt"***. Pictured on its cover was a father with his two young sons, his clothing and background set the stage as ancient Egypt. A parchment map and a Russian battle tank were imposed behind the family. Beyond a large red "X" painted on the map, nothing tied these seemingly unrelated images together to suggest buried treasure.

The back cover allowed the reader ominous clues about what lay inside. Three bulleted questions:

"WOULD YOU LIKE TO KNOW:"

- Where the greatest treasure in the world is buried?
- Why will Russia attack Israel?
- The secret behind the battle of Armageddon?

Pretty big questions for such a little book.

I need to qualify that dad was a teacher and a Bible scholar. He held advanced degrees in history and Greek.

When it came to the Bible, he knew his stuff. Biblical prophecy concerning the Apocalypse (the last days of this age of man) was a specialty and his position was often different from the popular view. His approach was original and unique and his results often reflected equally. The message conveyed in ***The Great Treasure Hunt*** didn't disappoint when it came to original and unique.

Biblical prophecy describes an event in which the armies of the world, led by *"Gog and Magog"* would invade Israel *"to take a spoil"*. The book's thesis was born with the question, *"What could Israel possibly possess in the last days that would make it such a prize for conquest that the world's armies would meet there to fight for the spoils?"* Israel's high-tech sector is respectable and her agricultural products are world-class but she doesn't possess wealth enough to warrant the world's avaricious interest to the point of invasion. Countries don't invade their neighbors for pomegranates and olive oil...but they do go to war over another kind of oil.

Petroleum. Light crude. The stuff the world runs on. Recent history has proven that oil is worth going to war over. It is feasible that Israel's enemies would invade to *"take a spoil"* if she possessed vast oil reserves. The problem however, is that Israel is an oil poor country. Fifty years of oil exploration and production in Israel have produced about 20 million barrels total. That's a little over two days of the oil production currently coming out of Saudi Arabia. Armies will go to war over oil, but not two days worth.

But what if a significant amount of oil were discovered in Israel; a really significant amount? Like fifty billion barrels? Fifty billion barrels is a lot of oil. At $50.00 per barrel it adds up to two and a half trillion dollars. Fifty billion barrels would satisfy Israel's current oil consumption needs for more than 500 years. With such a vast reserve Israel could become an oil exporting country. Israel, at fifty billion barrels of reserve, would rise into the top ten countries with greatest oil reserves. To gain some perspective, we should note that Saudi Arabia's current proven reserves are 261.7 billion barrels.

Fifty billion barrels of oil reserves by itself wouldn't make Israel a target for invading armies. Venezuela has 53 billion barrels of oil reserves; and as of this writing there have been no news reports of armies on the march to Venezuela to plunder her oil supply. Fortunately for Venezuela, she is not a small Jewish State surrounded by enemies sworn to wipe her off the face of the earth. Israel unfortunately is. The fact of her geographic location and the sentiments of her neighbors makes Israel's situation a little more interesting.

The Message

The Great Treasure Hunt was published in 1981; why republish it today, twenty-four years later? Its original message, like a seed planted in the hearts of a few believers back then has grown over the years into a tree, ready now to bear fruit. As a tree grows the seasons take their course. Spring, summer, fall and winter cast their effect on the tree's growth and the flavor of its fruit. In the seasons that have transpired since this seed was planted in 1981 world events have unfolded, preparing this message to bear fruit at its proper time and to its purposed effect.

This story is now much nearer its completion than when the first little paperback was released. The whole story didn't begin in 1981, however; its beginning was much further back. Two hundred million years ago, long before man's story on earth began, natural events were set in motion that would have profound implications today, even then preparing for the close of this present age. Nearly four thousand years ago a blessing was given and a promise was made by a father to his sons; a promise that his sons would *"suck honey from the rock"* and *"oil from the flinty rock."*

This promise, to the sons of Jacob, the people of Israel, is on the razor's edge of its realization. This book is the herald of this promise's fulfillment; and of its profound consequences.

Construction

The annotated and updated edition of the original manuscript, **Book I**, includes current events and explores the incredible implications waiting to explode in the Middle East when this treasure is brought to the surface. From the Middle East events will spread like a wind fanned fire beyond the region to the world at large. The realization of Jacob's promise will not just change the tenuous geo-political balancing act in the Middle East; it will become a crucible of decision, forcing the governments of the world to choose between Israel and her enemies.

Any additions to the original manuscript in Book I will appear inside of a shaded text box. This separation will denote information not included in the original manuscript.

Book II relates the stories of those who believed the message twenty-four years ago and threw their lives and fortunes into *__The Great Treasure Hunt__*. These stories bring us the results of more than two decades of searching for the treasure that was buried deep beneath the sands of Israel 200 million years ago. Their collective research and discoveries have provided scientific proof of the treasure's existence. These modern day treasure hunters have, just now, begun to tap its vast vault.

The Reason

As profound as the discovery of this treasure and its implications will be, there is another more important reason for this story; an eternal reason. This was not just a promise and a blessing given by Jacob to his sons. This is a promise and blessing given by God to his people. The story of oil in

Israel is part of the greatest story; the story of God's plan and purpose for man. The promise will be fulfilled. The oil will be brought to the surface. The abundance and implications of the discovery will become reality. But this will happen, not because Jim Spillman uncovered a thread of clues that reveal the treasure's location, or because faithful men have spent their lives and fortunes on its quest, or because Israel will benefit from the abundance oil will bring. This promise will be fulfilled because it is part of a greater promise. The promise that man will be reconciled with God and that this age will end and a new age will begin.

BOOK I

CHAPTER 1

An Eternal Covenant for the Israel of God

The Lord promised Abraham that he would make of him *"a great nation,"* that he would give him a land, a country that would be for his *"seed"*. Later on God told Moses about this *"promised land"* and that it would be flowing with milk and honey (Exodus 3:8). Moses was then directed to lead the children of Israel out of Egypt to the Promised Land, which finally he did. God had prepared this special land. He promised it to Abraham's *"seed"*. God always keeps his promises.

Moses encamped with the children of Israel at Paran and then sent twelve men secretly into Canaan to *"search"* it out. The spies returned with giant fruit and the report that indeed the land was flowing with milk and honey (Numbers 13:1–27). They also reported that there were giants in the land and that it was too dangerous to go into the land, *"promised"* or not. Only a small minority, two, Joshua and Caleb, gave a positive report regarding defeating the giants. Later, when the children of Israel did cross the Jordan and go into the land to possess it, God gave them strength and wisdom to defeat the giants.

God promised them rich land. He would help them *"possess it"*, was his added assurance. Beginning with Abraham and God's covenant with him, we see two focal points: the land and the people. God promised that he would bless and protect the people, and that he would give them the land "for an everlasting possession" flowing with *"milk and honey"* (Genesis 17:8 and Numbers 13:27).

> *The whole land of Canaan, where you are now an alien, I will give as an everlasting possession to you and your descendants after you; and I will be their God."* (Genesis 17:8 NIV)
>
> *They gave Moses this account: "We went into the land to which you sent us, and it does flow with milk and honey! Here is its fruit.* (Numbers 13:27 NIV)

Riches Underground

This covenant was an unconditional covenant. God said that he would do it, and true to his word of promise, he did it. The question of the land being rich on top has never been in doubt, but what of the natural resources under the ground? For most of history, agriculture was the basis of economy and livelihood. Land was valued for its surface richness. But since industry and super industry took over the world economy in the twentieth century, the riches under the surface of the land became far more valuable than the fertile soil. As I began this study my questions flowed forth:

> *"Lord, you know everything. You know what is going to happen before it happens. You knew that these last days were coming. You even spoke of the 'last days' in Genesis. You also knew that oil would be the single most valued commodity during the end times. Why would you have the children of Israel wander over some of the richest oil lands of the Middle East, and direct them to settle on oil poor real estate? It would be different if the land wasn't an 'everlasting possession'. It would be understandable. But you promised in your Word 600 years before the birth of Christ that 'Israel' would return in the 'latter*

days' and the land would produce even greater riches than before!" (Ezekiel 38:8).

After many days thou shalt be visited: in the latter years thou shalt come into the land that is brought back from the sword, and is gathered out of many people, against the mountains of Israel, which have been always waste: but it is brought forth out of the nations, and they shall dwell safely all of them. (Ezekiel 38:8)

I asked another question: *"Petroleum, how did you become so precious, so necessary and indispensable, when you were once nothing but grimy sludge?"*

CHAPTER 2

From Olive Oil to Petroleum

Oil has been use for various purposes for thousands of years. It is not known just when man began to use vegetable oil. Different plants were used, but olive oil proved to be the most versatile and desirable. It was used as a lubricant, an illuminant, for cooking and in medicine. When the use of oil is mentioned in the Bible, it is usually olive oil that is meant.

Bitumen, petroleum seepage on the surface of the ground, has also been used since man's history began. The Greek historian Herodotus, in the fifth century B.C., describes some of its uses and even where to find it.

There isn't much more that would be helpful in our study concerning the ancient use of oil. But the ancient understanding of *"what oil was"* is cogent to our search. Invariably when *"oil"* was used it was vegetable oil, mostly olive oil. Bitumen, when it could be found, was used, but was primitive in its unrefined state, and its uses were limited. The ancient mind never understood it as *"oil."* The concept of oil springing up from the ground was beyond their imaginings.

> There was no word for *"petroleum oil"* in ancient Israel. The Hebrew word for oil in the Old Testament was *"shemen"* meaning literally *"liquid grease"* or *"slimy stuff."* It was a generic term that could be used for any vegetable or animal fat. *"Zepheth"* is the ancient Hebrew word for bitumen. *"Zepheth"* means literally, *"softened asphalt."* As far as we know, ancient Hebrew's never related *"Zepheth"* to the concept of liquid petroleum.

The years passed, by the hundreds and then the thousands. Finally, in the 1800's discovery and use of petroleum became a reality. Oil was processed from shale rock in Scotland in 1850. However, it took American ingenuity and expertise to drill the world's first oil well, on August 27, 1859, at Titusville, Pennsylvania. What a timely discovery it was too, as the United States was in the beginnings of the Industrial Revolution – a revolution that would change the world! I wonder if the first drill-hand (roughneck) there in Titusville knew just how historic he was. This bubbling crude was to change man's welfare and his warfare. Wars could be won and countries lost because of this black grime that he was now wiping from his forehead. The future of the world was on his face!

From Titusville to Opecville

At first, petroleum was used for basic necessities such as fuel, lubricants, illuminants, and certain questionable medical purposes. By the time the new century rolled around (1900) many more uses and users were found. Hundreds of new oil wells were producing, and John D. Rockefeller, leading Standard Oil Company, was well on his way to becoming the *"richest man who ever lived"*.

Standard, as well as others, now began to search the world for new *"fields."* New strikes were discovered here and there, but none as large or as lucrative as the Middle East oil fields. The first oil strike was in Persia in 1908, and by the beginning of World War II the Middle East would be recognized as the greatest area of oil production in the world. As late as 1970 it could be said that 60% of the known oil reserves in the world were around and under the Persian-Arabian Gulf.

According to the U.S. Energy Information Administration, as of March 2005 proven oil reserves in the Persian Gulf nations were estimated at 729.3 billion barrels; about 57% of known world oil reserves. If you add in the former Soviet states and North African nations the percentage of total known reserves jumps to over 69% of world reserves.

Intense and sophisticated research and technology entered the *"oil business"* by the end of World War II. More petroleum products were discovered and quickly made available to a waiting public. Fuels, lubricants and illuminants were more refined. Solvents and surfacing materials were developed. Soap, detergents, fertilizers, insecticides, synthetic rubber for tires, man made fibers for clothing, paints, plastics, medicines, and even TNT were placed under the petroleum Christmas tree.

Every year saw not only new products from petroleum, but new users of the products. More wells were drilled, but the thirst for oil was vampiric. The veins of the earth were opened wider and deeper. The jugular in the Middle East was gushing from every incision, trying to quench an insatiable thirst that by the 1970's was demanding 1,500,000,000 gallons a day! Oil had become the single most important item of international trade.

> A barrel of oil is equal to 42 U.S. gallons. According to the U.S. Energy Information Administration, as of January 2005 world oil demand is at 84.9 million barrels per day (3,565,800,000 gallons), more than twice the world demand in the 1970's.

By 1960, certain oil-exporting countries felt the need of unity and concerted decision and action. In 1960, Saudi Arabia, Iran (Persia), Iraq, and Kuwait joined Venezuela as the charter members of OPEC (The Organization of Petroleum Exporting Countries). Thirty years later there would be many more members of OPEC.

Although demand was outrageous, world supplies were still higher than world demand, and the Saudi production was so high that the market held steady at around $2.00 a barrel all through the 60's. Gasoline was the greatest American bargain. Giant automobiles would guzzle this cheap fuel at 10 times the rate of any other country. The United States, drunk for so long on cheap gas, was about to experience its first case of the D.T.'s, for a blood feud that had broken out 3,900 years ago was about to break out on its bloodiest, most costly battle yet.

Prayer, Blood and Oil

The autumn of 1973 will go down in history as the *"beginning of the end."* As the Arabs launched their surprise attack against a truly surprised Israel, forces were being put into motion that would change the world! Aside from the grim reports of casualties and carnage of the intense war effort on Yom Kippur, world political and economic change was also triggered. The international body politic was in seizure.

The Arabs were fighting a *total* war. One of the most important things that they could do to cripple Israel was to cut off her oil supplies and the supply of any nation that aided her. On October 17, 1973, that is exactly what happened. Arab oil producers, in a Kuwait meeting, voted to reduce the output of oil. Some of the Arab states stopped altogether the export of oil to the United States.

The following month, on November 6, the Common Market, completely dependent on the free flow of Arab oil, endorsed a document calling for the Israelis to withdraw from occupied territories.

The United States, Israel's only strong ally, found herself increasingly isolated by world opinion. The other power blocs of the world were pro-Arab. The communist bloc was supplying arms to Syria and Egypt. The Pan-Arabian power bloc and its *"diplomatic"* tool OPEC were at war with Israel. Europe had spoken through the November 6th EEC statement and couldn't afford to befriend Israel. Japan and the non-aligned industrial nations desperately needed Arab oil. Some nations even felt that the U.S. had been the catalyst to start the Yom Kippur war. In the summer of 1973, during the debate of the Israel-Arab situation in the United Nations Security Council, the Council had been highly critical of Israel's continued occupation of Arab territory. The Council was moving toward a unanimous vote of censure, only to be stopped by the solitary veto of the United States.

The oil embargo of 1973, which produced a controlled supply of oil, signaled the end of petroleum's supply overage in the world. Demand now exceeded supply. This caused oil prices to double and then quadruple, and that was just the beginning! *"Peace"* was finally negotiated. The Arabs were richer. Both sides were wiser in the ways of war. Israel had lost world influence. Arabia, acting in concert, was now a world political power. Yom Kippur had brought a change in the balance of power. The United States and the Arabs were reconciled through the efforts of Henry Kissinger, but from this moment on America would not ever again be quite as *"pro-Israel"* as she had been. Her heart was in Jerusalem, but her gasoline credit card was lost somewhere in the shifting sands of Arabia.

Later Oil Discoveries

1979-81 brought new petroleum discoveries. There had been new wells drilled, to be sure, but these are not the discoveries to which I am referring. These three years had seen the phenomenal rise of crude oil prices. What was *"discovered"* is that we can no longer easily afford to buy gasoline for our cars or fuel to heat our homes.

1979 was called the year of crisis in the oil world. Iran was the reason. The overthrow of the Shah and the subsequent political upheaval caused Iran's huge oil production to staunch and then subside almost completely. The United States was hurt severely over this, as ten percent of her oil imports came from Iran. A check on prices at this time is most revealing. The first quarter of 1979 saw *Arabian light* crude oil selling at $13.34 a barrel. When the revolutionary Iranian students took the American hostages captive on November 4, 1979, *Arabian light* went to $41.00 a barrel – *African light* went to $43.00 (In 1972 this same oil sold for $2.00 a barrel)!

The United States has not purchased Iranian oil since 1979. Iran produces about 4 million barrels per day for world consumption. In June 2005 the *"spot price"* for crude oil topped $60 per barrel.

If 1979 was the *"year of crisis"*, 1980 was the *"year of surprise"*. The surprise came in the strange behavior of the oil markets. Experts were not able to tell just what was going to happen or to whom it was going to happen. 1981 saw more of the 1980 surprises. The supply had (temporarily) matched demand, but the prices continued to drift up! The money flowed rapidly from the West to the Middle East. The Morgan Bank ran several computer scenarios, and every one of them had OPEC with a surplus running into hundreds of billions of dollars, five hundred billion dollars in three years. That's the biggest amount of money ever let loose in the history of the world. All that money and all that oil!

Israel, on the other hand, apparently neither had money nor oil. She was hopelessly outnumbered, she was poor (inflation running over 100%), and she had no oil. She was constantly in danger of national extermination. If only she had oil!

Hidden Riches

Is there black gold, oil, in Israel? Did God deposit secret riches in the land of promise when He *"divided unto the nations their inheritance?"* Is that kind of thinking within the character of God? I, for one, believe that it is. Let us read Isaiah 45:3:

> *And I will give thee the treasures of darkness, and hidden riches of secret places, that thou may knowest that I, the Lord, which call thee by name, am the God of Israel.*

Verse four adds that he is doing this for *"Jacob my servant's sake."* Are *"the treasures of darkness, and hidden riches of secret places"* describing great oil deposits hidden deep in the earth? They could very well be, for this Bible text is addressed to Cyrus, not to Israel! Look at the first verses of Isaiah forty-five:

1. *Thus saith the Lord to his anointed, to Cyrus, whose right hand I have holden, to subdue*

nations before him; and I will loose the loins of kings, to open before him the two leaved gates; and the gates shall not be shut;

2. *I will go before thee, and make the crooked places straight: I will break in pieces the gates of brass, and cut in sunder the bars of iron:*

3. *And I will give thee the treasures of darkness, and hidden riches of secret places, that thou may knowest that I, the Lord, which call thee by name, am the God of Israel.*

4. *For Jacob my servant's sake, and Israel mine elect, I have even called thee by thy name: I have summoned thee, though thou hast not known me.*

We know that it was this very Cyrus who brought Persia into power in Babylon and then signed the decree of release for the captive Jews. Cyrus founded the Persian Empire. He was unknowingly used of God *"for Jacob my servant's sake."* But what about *"the treasures of darkness, and hidden riches of secret places?"* Does this mean that Persia had oil under its land? That must be exactly what it means, for it was in Persia in 1908 that the first oil well in the Middle East was drilled. If God rewarded Cyrus with an oil treasure for *"Jacob my servant's sake,"* would it not be commensurate with his character to bless Jacob in the same manner?

> The Hebrew word *"neft,"* (equivalent to the English word *"naphtha"*) came into existence as a result of the Israelites' Persian captivity around 500 BC. This was the first Hebrew word usage that meant specifically *"petroleum oil."* Apparently there is a connection between God's promise of *"the treasures of darkness, and hidden riches of secret places"* to Cyrus and petroleum!
>
> (source: Philip Mandelker)

If it is indeed within the character of God to act in this fashion, is it then to be found in the plan of God? In other words, if God would act this way, did he? The <u>only</u> place we can find an answer to that is in the Bible. But where would we start to look? Should we look up *"oil"* in Strong's Exhaustive Concordance and discover the first use of the word *"oil"* in the Bible and go from there? No, that wouldn't work at all, for as we have already stated, *"oil"* in the Bible meant either animal fat or olive oil. No Bible writer or character had the conceptual capacity to imagine oil coming from deep within the bowels of the earth. If we cannot trace oil by its name *per se* in the Bible, we must then depend on allusion and synonym, on symbol and type. Since this kind of tracing is subsidiary and not primary in its discovery and process, we must seek the primary trace line. If God did put oil in the sandy bosom of the Promised Land, He had a purpose for doing so. God's purpose would suggest a plan, and if we look hard enough we can discover his plan, and in the process see if there is petroleum present.

CHAPTER 3

Jacob: The Beginning

Although the unconditional covenant of God was given to Abraham, and it was to him that God promised to, *"make of thee a great nation"*, we will start with Jacob, his grandson. Jacob was the heir of God's promise to Abraham in every way; that is, what he said to Abraham he said to Jacob. The greater part of the Abrahamic covenant was futuristic in manifestation. It was in God's plan from the very beginning to use Jacob as a starting point, a national identity. This was clear even before Jacob was born, as he was yet in Rebekah's womb.

> *And the children struggled together within her; and she said, If it be so, why am I thus? And she went to inquire of the Lord.*
>
> *And the Lord said unto her, Two nations are within thy womb and two manner of people shall be separated from thy bowels; and the one people shall be stronger than the other people; and the elder shall serve the younger.*
>
> *And when her days to be delivered were fulfilled, behold, there were twins in her womb.*
>
> *And the first came out red, all over like an hairy garment; and they called his name Esau.*

> *And after that came his brother out, and his hand took hold on Esau's heel; and his name was called Jacob...*
>
> *Genesis 25:22 – 26*

The men were as different in their living as they were in their birthing. Esau was rough, an outdoor man. Jacob was smooth, an indoor man. Later Jacob outmaneuvered Esau, both for his birthright and for his father's blessing. The blessing that Isaac gave Jacob, albeit unknowingly, was essentially the same blessing that Abraham his father had given to him, who had in turn received it from God.

The name Esau was a pun on the word Edom meaning *"red"*. The name Jacob literally means *"heel-snatcher"*, a Hebrew term for one who supplants, or takes the place of another. either by force or treachery.

Intrigue followed Jacob as he finally got the wife he thought he had bargained for in the beginning. But the wife he loved, Rachel, was barren. Jacob wanted sons more than anything else. Leah, his first wife, the one he didn't even like, bore him a son. Finally, over a period of years and rather capricious family relationships involving his wives and their handmaids, Jacob ended up with twelve sons. Even Rachel, barren for so long, contributed with numbers eleven and twelve, Joseph and Benjamin. It was a good thing she did too, for without Joseph there would be no future for Israel.

Every Sunday school student knows the story of Joseph and his coat of many colors and his brothers' hatred; how he was sold into Egypt as a slave, but by God's intervention was made the number two man in all of Egypt. Then the famines came in Canaan and drove the children of

Israel down to Egypt. Egypt had experienced famine also, but Joseph, under God's direction, had stored more than enough food to last through the famine. The children of Israel were saved from starvation; Jacob and his sons were happily reunited with Joseph; and once again Jacob and his twelve sons were a unit, a nation in embryo.

Jacob Adopts Two Sons

Things went well for Jacob in Egypt, as the Bible testifies: *"And Israel dwelt in the land of Egypt, in the country of Goshen; and they had possessions therein, and grew and multiplied exceedingly."* (Genesis 47:27) All in all, Jacob lived in Egypt seventeen years before his death. As he was near death he called Joseph unto him:

> *...and said unto him, If now I have found grace in thy sight, put, I pray thee, thy hand under my thigh, and deal kindly and truly with me; bury me not I pray thee in Egypt.*
>
> *But I will lie with my fathers, and thou shalt carry me out of Egypt, and bury me in their burying place. And he said, I will do as thou hast said.*
>
> *...And Israel bowed himself upon the bed's head*
>
> *Genesis 47: 29 – 31*
>
> *And it came to pass after these things, that one told Joseph, Behold, thy father is sick; and he took with him his two sons, Manasseh and Ephraim.*
>
> *Genesis 48:1*

Joseph and his two sons went to Jacob's death bed where Jacob had a strange but wonderful surprise waiting for them. First, he blessed Joseph with:

> *Behold, I will make thee fruitful, and multiply thee, and I will make of thee a multitude of people; and I will give this land to thy seed after thee for an everlasting possession.*

> *Genesis 48:4*

Then came the surprise! Jacob, not even seeing Joseph's two sons (for his eyes were weak), told Joseph that he was going to adopt them as his own. Jacob said:

> *And now thy two sons, Ephraim and Manasseh, which were born unto thee in the land of Egypt before I came unto thee into Egypt, are mine; as Reuben and Simeon, they shall be mine.*

> *Genesis 48:5*

Why Would Jacob Adopt His Grandsons?

You might ask: *"Why would Jacob want to adopt two sons when he already had twelve? Why adopt them when he was dying?"* First and foremost, we are convinced that this was the plan of God, and God directed a dying Jacob to do this. But Jacob's human motivation is clear too. Jacob loved Joseph more than his other sons. He felt partly responsible for Joseph being sold into Egypt as a slave. Lastly, he was so very appreciative of Joseph for saving his family from starvation and then establishing them in Goshen land. Whatever the motivation was for Jacob's action, the result was dynamic and, as we will see later, strategically important. Ephraim and Manasseh were now to be considered Jacob's sons and would share in the inheritance as full-fledged sons, not once removed grandsons. As a simple matter of fact, Jacob was giving a double blessing to Joseph by issuing a two-for-one stock dividend! Jacob then put his right hand on Ephraim and his left hand on Manasseh and blessed them. He then turned to Joseph and said:

21. *Behold, I die; but God shall be with you, and bring you again unto the land of your fathers.*

22. *Moreover I have given thee one portion above thy brethren, which I took out of the hand of the Amorite with my sword and with bow.*

Genesis 48: 21 – 22

Manasseh was put before Jacob's right hand at the place of the first born; Ephraim was on Jacob's left. Jacob crossed his arms in order to bless Ephraim with his right hand and Manasseh with his left. This is the third incidence in Genesis when the blessing belonging to the eldest son is given to the younger.

In summary, when the children of Israel later would go in to take possession of their promised land, Joseph would receive two portions with the names of his sons Ephraim and Manasseh affixed to them

Jacob's Last Blessing

As Jacob was now very near death, he called all of his sons together to give out his last blessing. Genesis 49:1 declares this in very interesting fashion:

And Jacob called unto his sons, and said, Gather yourselves together, that I may tell you that which shall befall you in the last days!

(Exclamation mark author's)

Just imagine, Jacob is going to tell his sons what is going to befall them in the "*last days,*" and he is speaking

1600 years before Christ, almost four millennia before the last days!

Jacob proceeds to deal with each son individually in Chapter 49, but for our purpose we will focus only on Joseph and his blessing. Look with me at Genesis 49:22: *"Joseph is a fruitful bough, even a fruitful bough by a well; whose branches run over a wall."* Three things deserve notice in this verse. First, Joseph is to be fruitful. Second, he is a *"fruitful bough by a well"* (very interesting). Third, his blessings are so abundant that they *"run over the wall"*. This phrase tells us that indeed this blessing of Joseph's was to be plentiful and abundant. The fruit on the branches would be shared with those on the outside, those beyond the wall. I take this to mean other nations beyond Israel. Still, Joseph's blessing continues.

CHAPTER 4

The Head of Joseph

Blessings? Riches? Could they be the same? Is Joseph to be blessed to the extent that it could be called a national treasure? Has the Bible become an intricate treasure map for wealth that must be discovered in the *"last days"*? (Genesis 49:1). If so, are there clues right here in this chapter that might help us? Let's press on to Genesis 49:25:

> *Even by the God of thy father, who shall help thee; and by the almighty, who shall bless thee with blessings of heaven above, <u>blessings of the deep that lieth under</u>, blessings of the breasts, and of the womb:*

Most of this verse is self-explanatory, except the phrase: *"blessings of the deep that lieth under"*. What kind of blessing could this be? It says three things: It's a *blessing*, it's *deep*, and it *lieth under*. The verse by itself doesn't give us a real clue. By itself it is too oblique, too veiled.

According to the original Hebrew, Theologian Dr. Roger Luther comments, *"This blessing would be liquid, very deep...waiting for them, and it would be depressed...The words carry the meaning 'as a mass of water' – not necessarily water...Besides...God would somehow, some day use this buried resource in a prophetic way to draw, provide for, and unify His people in the land of promise."*

But we already have two things going for us that we can add to this verse. First, we know what treasure of blessing we are looking for – *oil*. Next, we have the clue in verse 22 that states: *"Joseph is a fruitful bough, even a bough by a well"*. Let's put our clues together. We are looking for oil, and oil comes from a well. The main reservoir or pool of oil down under the earth might be the *"blessings of the deep that lieth under"*.

"Too far-fetched," you say? Are we trying to make something fit that doesn't fit? A well could mean a supply of water, or this well could be a symbolic well denoting supply that brings abundance. *"It's too hard to even guess what the 'blessings of the deep that lieth under' means. It really doesn't tell us anything. It is too mysterious."* That is right. I would be the first to agree with that kind of reasoning, and with our initial conclusion. We already know that Joseph's blessing is written in code. It is cryptic and needs a key to unlock it. It was given for those days, but it wasn't to be understood until the time of its fulfillment – the *"last days"*. It is evident, however, that these scriptures won't stand by themselves to declare to us, *"there is oil in Israel."*

How we understand the Bible is limited to what kind of book we think it to be. We probably could agree that the Bible can be described as a collection of ancient wisdom and history written by men who lived a long time ago. But if that's as far as you go you may be missing the whole point and power of the book. It's true; the Bible is a collection of ancient wisdom and history written by men who lived a long time ago. But, limiting your understanding of what the Bible is to that statement is like saying the Mona Lisa is an assortment of colored grease smeared on a piece of canvas by a man who lived a long time ago. The statement is true but it misses the point, purpose and the power of the object.

If our understanding of the Bible is limited to the context and comprehension of the men who wrote its words we've missed the point, the purpose and the power of the Bible. If, however, we open our spiritual eyes and ears enough to imagine that the Bible is God's Word, God speaking to His people, whether they lived in the first days or live in the last days and that His message is as personal and relevant to us today as it was to Jacob's descendents 3,400 years ago we begin to understand that the Bible is more than a collection of ancient wisdom and history... a lot more. The Bible is literally *"God's Word."* That means God inspired the men who wrote the words of the Bible to write what they wrote. The Bible is a book of God's intent and purpose and message to man. The men wrote the words but it was God who directed the pen.

Genesis 49:26, the next verse, continues with more of Jacob's blessing for Joseph:

> *The blessings of thy father have prevailed above the blessing of my progenitors unto the utmost bound of the everlasting hills: they shall be <u>on the head of Joseph, and on the crown of the head of him that was separate from his brethren</u>.*

When Jacob declares here that *"The blessings of thy father have prevailed above the blessing of my progenitors"*, I believe he is referring specifically to Abraham and Isaac. Even though the unconditional covenant of God was first given to Abram (Genesis 12:2-3) and perpetuated through his son Isaac, it was Jacob who received the greater manifestation of the promise. The covenant is brought into focus in Jacob, named Israel. Jacob's name, Israel, was not only to be the name of the *"great nation"* that God had promised Abram (Genesis 12:2), but Jacob's sons were the tribes, or subsidiary social units, through whom the possessing of the land was to be effected. Indeed, Jacob's blessings did prevail above the blessings of his progenitors even in his own day. But the rest of verse 26 interests us far more in our treasure hunt! Here Jacob speaks of future blessings with *"they shall be"* on Joseph's head. He is actually telling us *where* the treasure (blessing) is! Look closely at the words again: *"they shall be on the <u>head of Joseph</u> and on the <u>crown of the head of him</u>..."* This is our first clue as to where the endowment is, rather than what it is. From this moment on we know that the bonanza we seek (oil) is to be found on Joseph's head. God has, in fact, anointed Joseph's head with oil! But what does that mean? Is it symbolic of cryptic or both? We know it can't be literal. I personally think that it is mostly cryptic. I feel it is only symbolic in the general sense in the meaning of anointing the head with oil. The Old Testament gives us several instances of this rite. Its usual meaning was to signify authority and blessing being conferred by a higher power. That is what I believe we see here. God is blessing Israel through this anointing of Joseph. However, our goal is not to discover veiled general meanings, but to find specific hidden liquid assets.

So then, if we can rely on the assumption that Genesis 49:26 tells us where the treasure is, what do we do now? It is clear that the verse is cryptic; that is, it is in code. We must unlock the meaning. To do this we must go on to see where this and the other two clues lead us. We must follow the scripture until it reveals to us its hidden meaning. We do have a couple of guides that we can follow personally with our clues. Our guides are named Joseph and Israel: Joseph the family and Israel the land. At this juncture Joseph is our guide.

Jewish tradition states that there are four ways to interpret Holy Scripture. Using the acronym PRDS - "Paradise" (the Hebrew alphabet contains no vowels).

P (Pay - p'shat) – "literal" (literally)

R (Reish - remez) – "hint" or "clue" (prophetically)

D (Dalet - drash) – "homiletic" or "example" (figuratively)

S (Samech - sod) –"secret" (cryptically)

* Philip Mandelker

Keeping Joseph in Sight

Armed with our three little clues, let us hurry on to follow Joseph after the death of his father Jacob. Genesis 50: 22 – 26 gives us the scriptural story of what happened:

And Joseph dwelt in Egypt, he, and his father's house: and Joseph lived an hundred and ten years.

And Joseph saw Ephraim's children of the third generation: the children also of Machir the son on Manasseh were brought up on Joseph's knees.

And Joseph said unto his brethren, I die: and God will surely visit you, and bring you out of this land unto the land which he sware to Abraham, to Isaac, and to Jacob.

And Joseph took an oath of the children of Israel, saying, God will surely visit you, and ye shall carry up my bones from hence.

So Joseph died, being an hundred and ten years old: and they embalmed him, and he was put in a coffin in Egypt.

Following the Sons

And so our guide, so quickly followed, is so quickly gone. We must, of course, follow his sons and their sons as we move ever closer to the mysterious *"blessings"* treasure. But before we grab our biblical spade to dig up another clue, let us consider the importance of Joseph's life from God's perspective. Perhaps we will then be better able to understand the unique role of Joseph in all of this.

Joseph Left a Heritage

Joseph had gone from prisoner to Prime Minister in Egypt. It was strictly providential that Joseph be in this high position at the time of famine so that his people might be preserved. Yet, we see another strategy of a provident God in getting the Israelites to leave Canaan at that time. They had to have the time and the opportunity to develop a national strength, so that when they took possession of the land they might have the sections properly allotted to the tribes, and thus prevent the tribes as tribes from becoming disintegrated by settling in different parts of the country. It was most important that the tribes be kept together and be properly located (more on this later).

It was also necessary that the Israelites be taken out of Canaan so that they would not mingle and intermarry with the idolatrous races of the people who also dwelled in Canaan. The famine forced them out of Canaan into Egypt where they were put in a separate place called Goshen. The Hyksos nation had conquered Egypt before this time, and so there was a Hyksos Pharaoh on the throne during Joseph's sojourn there. The importance of this lies in the fact that the Egyptians hated the Hyksos and would have nothing more than was absolutely necessary to do with them. Joseph, a foreigner, was favored by the Hyksos Pharaoh, a foreigner to the Egyptians, and so the idolatrous Egyptians rejected him and his people out of hand. This preserved the children of Israel from associating with them and their paganism. This Egyptian experience was also a fulfillment of prophecy that was given to Abram.

> *And he said unto Abram, Know of a surety that thy seed shall be a stranger in a land that is not theirs, and shall serve them; and they shall afflict them four hundred years.*

Genesis 15:3

He also promised in verse 14 that *"afterward shall they come out with great substance."*

Joseph's life was integral in its purity and its power to the preservation, development, and preparation of Israel relative to the possession of the Promised Land. It is because of this, I believe, that God allotted a double portion of land in Canaan to Joseph, and anointed Joseph's head with the oil of blessing and prosperity.

Recapping the Clues

Let us now briefly recap our *"clue"* scriptures to bring us up to date and prepare us for the next step toward the mysterious *"X"* on our treasure map. First we have Genesis 49:22 that tells us that *"Joseph is a fruitful bough...by a well"*. Could this possibly allude to a fountain of oil that would some day spring up out of Joseph's land? Second, Genesis 49:25 speaks of the *"blessings of the deep that lieth under..."* Is the *"deep that lieth under"* a great pool of petroleum? Third, Genesis 49:26 points us to the place of Joseph's blessings. It says that they will be found *"...on the head of Joseph, and on the crown of the head of him that was separate from his brethren."* This makes it simple, yet hard. We have discovered the place of Joseph's blessings, the top of his head. Now all we have to do is find his head!

*(Author's note): *At this moment you may be mumbling, "This is ridiculous; this sounds like some mad, mad, mad world television script – long on fantasy and nonsense, but short on fact." I couldn't agree more, for that is exactly what I said! One of my biggest problems was this: Is it sensible to think that an ancient civilization would actually write something in code that would not be decoded until modern time? The idea was so remote, but then I thought of the Rosetta Stone.*

Consider the Rosetta Stone

Ancient Egypt wrote special messages that were carved in stone. The pyramids of famous Pharaohs provide numerous examples. The cryptic writings are called hieroglyphics (temple writings). Hieroglyphics guarded the treasure of ancient Egypt for millenniums. Not until the key was discovered was the great treasure house opened. It was 1799 that the key, the Rosetta Stone, was accidentally found. It was someone in Napoleon's invading French army who uncovered the great basalt rock. It was found at the Rosetta mouth of the great Nile River, hence its name. There was a Greek inscription on the Rosetta Stone, and it was this writing that gave the key to the French scholar Champollion who deciphered the Egyptian hieroglyphics. It was so easy to unlock the treasures of millennia _after_ the key had been found and applied. If the ancient Egyptians used the principles of coded language for their own veiled purpose, couldn't God use the same principle (at about the same time in history) for His own purpose? If the Egyptian hieroglyphic key, the Rosetta Stone, was not presented publicly until the 1800's, is it too hard for us to imagine the discovery and presentation of the key to this Bible code in the 1900's? Remember what Jacob said to his sons at the time that he called them together to give them his final blessing: *"Gather yourselves together, that I may tell you that which shall befall you in the last days"* (Genesis 49:1).

CHAPTER 5

Israel, the Land

It is time for us to give our guide Joseph a brief rest, and follow for a while our second guide, Israel the land. We remember that Jacob (Israel) made his son Joseph vow that he wouldn't bury him in Egypt, and Joseph, true to his vow, took his father's body back to Canaan and buried him at Machpelah with his father and mother, and grandfather and grandmother.

When it was time for Joseph to die, he demanded an oath also. Joseph's oath was not with one of his sons, but was with the *"children of Israel"* (Genesis 50:25). He knew that God was going to allow the children of Israel to stay in Egypt only for a prescribed time. When the fullness of time would come, they would leave Egypt and possess Canaan. Joseph, unlike Jacob, was content to have his bones remain in Egypt until that time. Joseph made the Israelites promise that when God did *"visit"* Egypt to direct them to Canaan, they would take his bones with them that he might also rest with his fathers. The stage is now set for the *"Exodus"*.

And Joseph died, and all his brethren, and all that generation.

And the children of Israel were fruitful, and increased abundantly, and multiplied, and waxed exceeding mighty; and the land was filled with them.

Now there arose up a new king over Egypt, which knew not Joseph.

And he said unto his people, Behold, the people of the children of Israel are more and mightier than we:

Come on, let us deal wisely with them; lest they multiply, and it come to pass, that, when there falleth out any war, they join also unto our enemies, and fight against us, and so get them up out of the land.

Exodus 1:6 - 10

From Egypt to the Jordan

The 400 years of Israel's sojourn were almost accomplished. Jacob's family, which had come into Egypt as seventy souls, weak and needy, was now ready to leave as a strong tribal nation.

Moses was born, grew strong, and was schooled by the God of Abraham, Isaac, and Jacob for the arduous task that lay before him. If Joseph, the last great leader of the children of Israel, was the preserver, Moses, the next great leader, was the deliverer. He brought them out of Egypt, through years of futile wandering, to the turbulent Jordan, the river of no return. Moses, now 120 years old, had almost finished his heavenly assignment. He must now pass on the tribal blessings, given hundreds of years ago by Jacob, to the twelve tribes of Israel. It was now time to commission Joshua to lead the tribes in the invasion of Canaan and possess Jacob's inheritance. The land, the tribal blessings; each was dependent on the other,

Once again it is time for us to look closely at our treasure map. We are closer than ever to the mysterious *"X"* and the richest buried treasure in the history of the world!

The Song of Moses

Scripturally our treasure story picks up again in Deuteronomy Chapter 32. This chapter gives us the song of Moses, his swan song, if you please. It was given to all the people for edification and warning. It was his last great sermon. He was, even now, passing the baton of responsibility and authority to Joshua, the next great leader of Israel. For our purposes let us direct our attention to Deuteronomy 32:8 - 13:

> *When the Most High divided to the nations their inheritance, when he separated the sons of Adam, he set the bounds of the people according to the number of the children of Israel,*

> *For the Lord's portion is his people; Jacob is the lot of his inheritance.*

> *He found him in a desert land, and in the waste howling wilderness; he led him about, he instructed him, he kept him as the apple of his eye.*

> *As an eagle stirreth up her nest, fluttereth over her young, spreadeth abroad her wings, taketh them, beareth them on her wings:*

> *So the Lord alone did lead him, and there was no strange god with him.*

> *He made him ride on the high places of the earth, that he might eat the increase of the fields; and he made him to suck honey out of the rock, and <u>oil out of the flinty rock:</u>*

The Inheritance of the Nations

The opening statement in verse eight is one of the most dramatic statements in scripture: *"When the Most High divided to the nations their inheritance..."* As our imagination releases and our thoughts run free, two questions leap forth. *When* did the Most High divide to the nations their inheritance? *"What"* is a nation's inheritance? Let's consider the second question first. *"What"* is a nation's inheritance? I am convinced that it is its land, both the richness of its topsoil, and the wealth deposited deep under the soil. All physical wealth (or inheritance) must come from the land in some form or other, so it seems logical to conclude that the inheritance is the land.

> The original Hebrew text seems to agree that the land is the inheritance. The Hebrew word *"chebel"* is translated into the English word *"lot"* in verse nine. *"Chebel"* literally means *"measuring line"*, *"district"*, *"region"*, or *"country"*. All definitions for *"chebel"* are geographic in context. This word key will unlock the clues ahead.

It could be argued, I suppose, that people are a nation's inheritance, but this doesn't seem to be very logical. An inheritance is something of value passed on from one generation to another. People do not inherit people. Children don't inherit parents, but rather what the parents possess. It might also be said that the inheritance of a nation might be a spiritual thing, but this, too, seems unreasonable. God told Moses that He was *"I am"*, not *"I was"* or *"I will be"*. Each generation and each person of a generation has the responsibility of personally relating to a personal God who dwells in his fullness in that generation. In the Bible some generations are called *"sinful"*; none are called *"righteous"*. Spiritual kinship is a personal *"now"*, not a national *"then"*.

My conclusion is that a nation's inheritance is its land, or more specifically, its natural resources. In Bible times, during the history of both Testaments, usable natural resources were either on the surface or close to the surface of the land. Some of those resources were lakes, rivers, shallow wells, fertile soil, trees, and even minerals from shallow mines. The very thought of something valuable being extricated from deep within the earth, such as *"the deep that lieth under,"* was beyond conception. There were no tools, no technological capacity available for such a project. As we have discussed, this technology didn't come until the end of the nineteenth century. Yet, if the *"deep that lieth under"* is oil, this kind of chronological timetable would fit perfectly. Remember what Jacob said in Genesis 49:1? He gathered his sons together to tell them what would befall them *"in the last days."* These are the "last days." So time wise, the fit is a good one.

When Was This Inheritance Given?

Now let us consider the first question. *"When"* did the Most High divide to the nations their inheritance? Long before Adam was created God was at work in the physical creation. If we count back through the generations of Adam to the time of Adam's creation we end up *circa* 4,000 – 5,000 years before the birth of Christ. We know that the world is much older than that. In fact, there is evidence that a pre-Adam people existed. We know, by countless fossils, that huge mammals roamed the earth. These animals have been extinct at least for the duration of written history. We know, too, that huge vegetation forests were located in various parts of the world during this pre-history period. But at some moment long ago in the ether-like past of pre-Adam, there was a great cataclysm, a general chaos. I believe that not only did it happen that way, but that it happened as a direct result of Lucifer being cast down from his exalted place in the heavens to the earth. He was condemned to live on this planet until the time of his ultimate judgment. I am convinced that planet earth came under the scope and span of this judgment, and a catastrophic upheaval of cosmic proportions was set into motion. How long this lasted isn't even guessable, but when it was finished much of the earth was inside-out. In places, what had been surface was deeply submerged. Great forests, gigantic swamps, giant animals innumerable were volcanically plowed under. What had been formed was now without form. What was alive was now dead. For *"the earth was without form, and void, and darkness was upon the face of the deep."* (Genesis 1:2)

It seems feasible to think that between Genesis 1:1 and 1:2 there was a chaotic period, this very period that we have just described. Verse one says: *"In the beginning God created the heaven and the earth."* Verse two continues with the dark statement that the earth was *"without form, and void."* As God could not create an earth *"without form, and void,"* then something disruptive, something chaotic must have happened between the first and second verses. This could explain the dinosaur fossils, the mountain ranges, the ocean troughs, the earth rifts, the tectonic plates, and the huge lakes of highly compressed animal and vegetable matter couched deep in the earth that we now call petroleum.

According to the latest seismic studies, geologists believe that Israel's oil lies in a Mohilla reef formation some 14,000 feet below the surface. This reefal structure is located in the *"upper Triassic"* region geologists believe to be over 200 million years old. God *"divided to the nations their inheritance,"* a long, long time ago.

Jacob Is the Center

Returning now to Deuteronomy 32:8 – 13, let's look at verse nine. In the last part of the verse Moses tells us that *"Jacob is lot of his inheritance."* For us, the name Jacob is important here because it was with Jacob that we found our first clues, oblique as they were. Moses, in his death song, almost half a millennium after Jacob, is referring back to

Jacob, and to the subject of Jacob's blessing for his sons. Later we will see how Moses actually passes the blessings of Jacob along to the tribes, even expanding the meaning and value of them. Suffice for us now to see that Moses is discussing Jacob. In verses 9 - 12 he speaks of his special relationship with God; while in verse 13 he gives us our long-awaited next clue - and it is a dandy! Look closely at the last half of verse 13, *"...and he made him to suck honey out of the rock, and oil out of the flinty rock!"*

Sucking Oil!

Oil! Could it mean olive oil, the only oil known to Moses? No, of course not! It would be absurd to speak of sucking oil out of a certain type of rock when everyone there knew that oil came from crushed olives. Someone might question here: *"Isn't it just as absurd to think of sucking honey out of a rock when everyone knew honey came from beehives?"* The answer to that is *"yes, it is just as absurd,"* but it doesn't mean *"bee honey;"* it means *"earth"* honey, a synonym for petroleum. What we have here is a Hebrew parallelism, common in the Bible. Here, honey and oil mean the same thing! The first is symbolic; the second is literal. A simple way to prove this is to locate the verb of the object honey, and of the object oil. Notice that there is one verb, suck, for both objects. Of course, neither honey nor olive oil was sucked into use. Even more interesting is the observation that if you wanted to use the word pump in this context, that the Hebrew word here translated suck is the word that you would use.

"Oil out of the flinty rock," remained a phrase of mystery for thousands of years, that is, until 1850, when a process was developed for extracting oil out of shale (flinty rock?).

"Suck" in this passage is *"yanaq"*, the same Hebrew word used for a baby nursing; literally sucking milk from its mother's breast. There are two other Hebrew words that could be translated *"suck"* but their meanings are closer to *"drink up"*. If Moses were speaking of *"drinking up"* olive oil and honey why would use the word for *"suckle"* rather than the words meaning *"to drink up"*? Perhaps he was conveying a different meaning. He had no word for petroleum and he had no concept of the mechanical pump. If Moses wanted to describe *"pumping petroleum"*, concepts of which he hadn't the faintest idea, it's conceivable that the only words he had to describe the picture he had been given by God were *"suck honey out of the rock, and oil out of the flinty rock."* Let's say you're willing to consider for a moment that *"shemen"* might be used for petroleum and *"yanaq"* might be used to describe pumping something to the surface. This passage includes *"honey"*. Surely there's not some other Hebrew word for honey? Sorry, *"D^{e}bash"* is the only Hebrew word for honey. Its literal meaning *"to be gummy"* or *"syrupy"*, honey was named after its physical properties; not because it was sweet or came from bees. If Moses meant *"drink up"* olive oil and bees' honey why would he say they would *"suckle"* them *"out of the rock"* and *"out of the flinty rock?"* Using these words individually, a case might be made that Moses was just being poetic; but collectively you've got to wonder if he may have meant something else. If Moses was trying to accurately describe an understanding given to him by God that, in the last days, an oily, syrupy, sticky substance, maybe amber in color, was to be sucked from the ground (the rock) and he had no words for or concept of petroleum oil being pumped from deep underground, could he use the word *"yanaq"* (to suck) instead of pump and the words *"d^{e}bash"* (gummy syrupy stuff) or *"shemen"* (oil) instead of petroleum? ...Maybe.

So Moses, in his song to the nation Israel, gives us the clearest, the strongest clue yet, in our search for this *"buried treasure"*. Ah, the Bible, what a treasure map it is! But wait, we mustn't get too excited yet. The best is yet to come. We must resume our search for the mysterious *"X"*, for it is there that we will dig (drill) for the treasure.

Moses' Blessing

Deuteronomy 33 is the chapter detailing the blessing of Jacob given by Moses. It is here that we shall finally discover our mysterious *"X"*.

Verse one is our scriptural first step: *"And this is the blessing, wherewith Moses the man of God blessed the children of Israel before his death."* This *"blessing"*, this Godly inheritance, is the same blessing given by Jacob just before his death hundreds of years before. It was part and parcel of the covenant made by God with Abram two generations before Jacob. Jacob's blessing was much more definitive than Abraham's covenant, and now Moses' blessing is much more definitive and precise than was Jacob's. In other words, God didn't give all the information to Abraham or to Jacob, but rather gave as much as was needed at the time. Now, as the children of Israel are actually about to go over Jordan and into the land, he is giving a broader and deeper explanation of the tribal inheritance. This progressive giving of illumination and knowledge is easier for us to understand when we know that the land is the people's inheritance. For the children of Israel this was graphically true. The closer they got to the land the more they needed to know about its possession, its purpose and its properties.

Deuteronomy 33:6 is where the personal blessing begins. As Reuben is the eldest, it starts with him. Verse seven tells us of Judah's blessing, and verse eight begins the explanation of the blessing of Levi. However, those three tribes are not cogent to our study, so we must nod in recognition and resolutely press on past them. We are about to come upon some very unique and interesting details of our treasure map. The first one is so unobtrusive, so left-handed, that it might go unnoticed by even a careful reader. Let's look at Benjamin, the baby, the youngest of Jacob's brood.

Between His Shoulders?

And of Benjamin he said, The beloved of the Lord shall dwell in safety by him; and the Lord shall cover him all day long, and he shall dwell between his shoulders.

Deuteronomy 33:12

Actually there are only two cryptic phrases in this verse; the rest of the verse is easily understood. The first phrase that catches our attention and makes us question is *"...and the Lord shall cover him all the day long..."* What does that mean? Is it symbolic or is it cryptic? Is it symbolic, as is the use of *"cover"* in Psalm 91:4: *"He shall cover thee with his feathers, and under his wings shalt thou trust...?"* I don't think that it is symbolic. I believe that it is both cryptic and literal. This position cannot be proven by verse twelve itself, but we will find that the context of the chapter will provide enough evidence. Sufficient here to state that *"to cover"* means to put something over the top of something or someone. It sounds like rather a childish explanation, doesn't it? Yet, we will see that it will be more cryptic than pedantic.

The questions continue. What in the realm of common sense or imagination does it mean when it states in verse twelve that *"...he shall dwell between his shoulders?"* Between *whose* shoulders will Benjamin be dwelling? The previous phrase says *"...and the Lord shall cover him all the day long..."* Should we use grammatical assumption and conclude that Benjamin is to dwell between the Lord's shoulders? This would be very hard to deal with. It's not difficult for us to understand the symbolism of *"the hand of the Lord"* or *"the voice of the Lord"*, but *"between his shoulders"* is just too much. Yet, *"between his shoulders"* has to mean something. Let's see if we can dig it out. Shoulders…shoulders…they are a part of the human anatomy; this we know. Just a moment! Didn't we have another part of the anatomy mentioned in one of our clues? Joseph's *head*! Our third clue (Genesis 49:26) was that *"the blessings…shall be on the <u>head</u> of Joseph."* Now we have two parts of the anatomy named in our clue search: "*head*" and "*shoulders*" - not much to go on, but at least they connect! Even more difficult to handle is the concept of Benjamin "*dwelling*" between his shoulders. It doesn't make any literal sense for someone to "*dwell*" between someone's shoulders. Dwelling supposes a place, a dwelling place. How large would this place have to be? Well, the last numbering of Benjamin's tribe is listed in Numbers 26:41*: "These are the sons of Benjamin after their families: and they that were numbered of them were forty and five thousand and six hundred."* If the tribe of Benjamin was to dwell between shoulders, it would take some pretty broad shoulders! The more we look at this the more apparent it becomes that *"…between his shoulders"* has to do with a portion of land, not a portion of someone's body. The word *"shoulders"* could only be a hint, a clue to the identification and location of the land that the tribe of Benjamin was about to inherit. Let's go back, right here, to the question, *"whose shoulders?"* I don't think it accidental that verse twelve speaks of Benjamin and verse thirteen begins the explanation of Joseph's blessing. The twelve tribes are not listed for blessing in chronological order. I believe it will become apparent later that the continuity of verses twelve and thirteen have a deeper meaning than mere chance. We know that Joseph and Benjamin were full brothers, the sons of Rachel. All of the other brothers were half brothers born of three separate mothers. Still, it appears that the connection of

Joseph and Benjamin in the blessing order has a wiser design than the affection of brotherhood. Simply put, it is Joseph's shoulders that Benjamin is to *"dwell between."* *"Ridiculous."* you say! Smile on, for the meaning cometh. Ah, ah, just teasing, stay with me.

Joseph's Head Returns

Deuteronomy 33:13-16 describes Joseph's blessing in the new land.

> *And of Joseph he said, Blessed of the Lord be his land, for the precious things of heaven, for the dew, and for the deep that coucheth beneath.*
>
> *And for the precious fruits brought forth by the sun, and for the precious things put forth by the moon.*
>
> *And for the chief things of the ancient mountains, and for the precious things of the lasting hills.*
>
> *And for the precious things of the earth and fulness thereof, and for the good will of him that dwelt in the bush:* <u>*let the blessing come upon the head of Joseph*</u>*, and upon the top of the head of him that was separated from his brethren.*

The opening phrases of verse thirteen keep us in focus as we faithfully plod on: *"And of Joseph he said, Blessed of the Lord be his land..."* Joseph's *"land"* has been blessed by God. How can land be blessed? What is the difference between *"blessed"* and unblessed land? It seems to me that the only way to *"bless"* is to makes it rich, both on the surface and under the surface. It also seems to me that that is exactly what God did in his blessing of Joseph's land.

Let's take a look at these same verses in the New American Standard Version, as it makes it easier for us to understand this section:

> *And of Joseph he said, Blessed of the Lord be his land, With the choice things of heaven, with the dew, and from the deep lying beneath, and with the choice yield of the sun, And with choice produce of the months. And with the best things of the ancient mountains, And with the choice things of the everlasting hills, And with the choice things of the earth and its fulness, And the favor of Him who dwelt in the bush. Let it come to the head of Joseph, And to the crown of the head of the one distinguished among his brothers.*
>
> *Deuteronomy 33:13-16 NASB*

The Blessings of the Other Brothers

"Jacob's blessing" for Simeon and Levi are non-blessings, judgments. Later, we will see in Deuteronomy 33 that Moses doesn't even mention Simeon's name in his blessing. Levi's not allowed to possess any tribal territory at all but Simeon will finally acquire tribal land.

Since Zebulun, Issachar, and Joseph, and possibly Asher are blessed by Jacob through their land, let's follow these four tribes in Deuteronomy 33 and Moses' blessing. Verse thirteen declares:

> *And of Joseph he said, Blessed of the Lord be his land, for the precious things of heaven, for the dew, <u>and for the deep that coucheth beneath.</u>*

"Blessings of the Deep that Lieth Under"

This is very much like Genesis 49:25 which promises *"...and by the Almighty, who shall bless thee with blessings of heaven above, blessings of the deep that lieth under..."* There is no doubt that *"the deep that lieth under"* and *"the deep that coucheth beneath"* are one and the same. Because there was no technology to extract anything from *"the deep"* in the days of Jacob or Moses, neither they nor the children of Israel knew what it was that Joseph was inheriting. It is strong enough for us, however, to use as our fourth clue to lead us to the treasure of oil. Verses fourteen and fifteen speak of blessings, but more of the variety that would be found on top of the ground, but Deuteronomy 33:16 is a different matter entirely. Look at the last half of the verse: *"...let the blessing come upon the head of Joseph, and upon the top of the head of him that was separated from his brethren."* We have clue number five, or if you will, a confirmation of clue number three.

Another Hebrew Parallelism

The head of Joseph has indeed returned! It's not the only returnee, for the Hebrew parallelism presents itself once again also. Remember when we discussed Deuteronomy 32:13: *"And he made him to suck honey out of the rock, and oil out of the flinty rock?"* We have one verb, *"suck",* but two objects, *"honey"* and *"oil."* The action is the same and the objects *"honey"* and *"oil"* are the same, really synonyms. Hence, Hebrew parallelism.

Verse sixteen of chapter 33 has the same construction, a parallelism. *"Let the blessing come upon the head of Joseph"* parallels with *"and upon the top of the head of him that was separated from his brethren."* This particular parallelism is much easier to identify than is the one in 32:13, yet is just as important to our treasure hunt. We have said that the first part of the parallel is usually symbolic and the last part is usually literal. Here, then, we have the symbolism of Joseph's head being anointed with oil by God. The next part of the parallel is much the same as the first, except it designates more precisely just where the blessing (oil) is to be found - *"the top of the head."* Not the back or the front or the side of the head, but the top is where the blessing is to be found. A better translation of this word for *"top"* is *"crown"*. The New American Standard Bible uses the word *"crown"* in this verse, as we noticed in the printed translation. Remember that the companion verse of Genesis 49:26 uses *"crown"* instead of *"top"* also. At the moment this does not appear to be very important, but later it will spring forth dramatically as a very necessary part of our map.

> *"Two things quickly appear: First, this land blessing for Joseph would be near the top of the land grant and, more specifically, on the part that would correspond to the resting place of a crown on a man's head [directly on the top]. Secondly, this blessing was destined by God for a specific tribe and geographical area set aside by God for a specific divine purpose."*
>
> Dr. Roger Luther

Joseph is Represented by His Two Sons

Perhaps you noticed that we left verse seventeen out of our scripture printout in both the King James Version and the New American Standard Bible. This was purposeful. The verse still applies to Joseph, but must be explained separately. The verse says:

> *His glory is like the firstling of his bullock, and his horns are like the horns of unicorns: with them he shall push the people together to the ends of the earth: and they are the ten thousands of Ephraim, and they are the thousands of Manasseh.*

This verse continues the description of Joseph's blessing, but is somewhat different from the preceding verses in that the blessing is transitioned to Ephraim and Manasseh, his two sons. *"His glory is like the firstling of his bullock"* is a poetic allusion to this very thing. Finally, the transition is made by the end of verse seventeen with *"...and they are the ten thousands of Ephraim, and the thousands of Manasseh"*. Jacob did not mention either Ephraim or Manasseh in his blessing in Genesis 49, but Moses here in Deuteronomy 33 has a little different situation. Jacob has already adopted his two grandsons in Genesis 48 so that they would receive Joseph's blessing when Israel returned to the land. Now that Israel had returned to the land under the leadership of Moses, and he was perpetuating and defining Jacob's original blessing, it was necessary to use Joseph's name in conjunction with that of Ephraim and Manasseh. There was to be no tribal land named *"Joseph"*. Joseph would receive twice the inheritance of the other brothers, but it would be the names of his two sons that would identify the two portions.

> *"It is highly possible, and very probable...that God has additional plans in the future that include the land, the product, and people from the land that was once promised to the sons of Joseph! If God used the productivity and power from the land of Joseph, to conquest and drive away once, he certainly can use it again! Whatever comes out of that land will have might and this might will be of the utmost quality and quantity."*
>
> Dr. Roger Luther

What we must understand from this moment on is that when we speak of Joseph in our hunt for the treasure, we will see Ephraim and Manasseh.

"Rejoice in Thy Going Out"

Jacob's fifth son was Issachar and his sixth son was Zebulun. Leah was the mother of both. As both boys were so close in birth and in life, it is fitting that they be close in their inheritance also. Deuteronomy 33:18 - 19 demonstrates this:

> *18 And of Zebulun he said, Rejoice, Zebulun in thy going out; and Issachar, in thy tents.*
>
> *19 They shall call the people unto the mountain; there they shall offer sacrifices of righteousness; for they shall suck of the abundance of the seas, and of the treasures hid in the sand.*

What we see immediately in verse nineteen are the last two phrases. Before we discuss what the verses are saying, let's notice that our friend the Hebrew parallelism has returned once more. In fact, it reminds us of the first parallel we considered (Deuteronomy 32:13), that speaks of sucking *"honey out of the rock, and oil out of the flinty rock"*. The same word, *"suck"*, is used in both verses. There was, of course, no word for *"pump"* in those days, as the idea and the technology for pumping was still thousands of years in the future. Yet, if we were to write these verses today we would say *"pump"*, not *"suck"*. The next question begs an answer. What is it that one could suck (pump) out of the seas and out of the sand? You don't pump fish out of the seas; they must be netted or hooked. Consider the sand. The idea is just as strange and difficult to comprehend. What in the world could be pumped out of the sand? I think that the answer on both counts is the same: oil. In recent years offshore oil-drilling has become a normal activity. It looked a little different to begin with, but today seeing an oil rig standing in hundreds of fathoms of ocean water is commonplace. Sucking *"of the abundance of the seas"* is a *"last days"* phenomenon. The sea and the sand, both known petroleum depositories, go together as closely as Zebulun and Issachar in giving us our next vital clue as to where the great treasure is buried. The descendants of Zebulun and Issachar, indeed, will have much to rejoice about.

> Oil geologists believe that the lion's share of oil and gas reserves to be discovered in Israel lie offshore in the Mediterranean Sea. A significant amount of Israeli offshore territory is already under oil exploration permit, license, or lease today.

Gad, of the Torn Arm

One of the strangest passages of scripture in the Bible is in Deuteronomy 33:20. Let's look at the whole verse:

> *And of Gad he said, Blessed be he that enlargeth Gad: he dwelleth as a lion and teareth the arm with the crown of the head.*

The last two phrases are certainly not literal, and they are much too strange to be symbolic, so they must be cryptic. If they are, they fit well with the anatomy code key that we previously introduced.

> The NIV translation may give us a clearer picture of verse 20 and the first part of 21, *"Blessed is he who enlarges Gad's domain! Gad lives there like a lion, tearing at arm or head. He chose the best land for himself; the leader's portion was kept for him..."*

We will talk more of this later, when it is time to decipher the code and apply the meaning. Take heart, patient treasure hunters, for the moment draweth nigh.

Asher Dips His Foot in Oil

Deuteronomy 33:24 is a very special verse for us:

And of Asher he said, Let Asher be blessed, with children; let him be acceptable to his brethren, <u>and let him dip his foot in oil</u>.

Here it is, as clear a verse to designate oil in Israel that you could ever ask for. Two things in this verse must not escape our notice. First, the anatomy code is continued: *"and let him dip his foot in oil."* Next, the word *"oil"* is used in such a way that we know that it couldn't mean olive oil. It has to mean petroleum. Here someone might ask: *"I agree that it couldn't be olive oil - that wouldn't make sense but don't you think that calling it petroleum is stretching the point a bit?"* If verse twenty-four was the only verse we had telling us of Asher's oil blessing, we could all ask that same question, but look at verse twenty-five! *"<u>Thy shoes shall be iron and brass</u>; and as thy days, so shall thy strength be."* Aren't those first seven words marvelous, unique and thought-bending all at the same time? Asher has a foot that is to be *dipped in oil*, and has shoes that are to be made of *"brass and iron!"*

"Dipping the foot in oil points to a land flowing with oil. The text speaks of shoes made of iron and brass and he is to plunge one of these feet into something. Although the [Biblical] Jews would not be miners, the words definitely point to rich natural resources awaiting them in the land... scripture teaches that this tip area of Asher's foot ...contains some of the greatest wealth of all the land promised to Abraham's children and directed specifically to the tribe of Asher. Secondly, part of this wealth is mineral and part of it was (or is) in liquid form."

Dr. Roger Luther

Do you know that oil derricks are made of brass and iron? Brass against iron does not cause sparks as iron against iron does. So then, the combination of brass and iron is used so that sparks will not ignite an oil well fire!

A few years ago my wife and I were in Singapore. As we boarded the 747 to come home to Los Angeles, we noticed a large group of Americans in the ticket line with us. They were Texans, and they were friendly, but mostly they were happy to be going home. As we talked with them on the plane we found out the most interesting story of why they were in Singapore. They had just flown into Singapore from Java, they told us, where they had extinguished a huge oil well fire. The fire had been so large and so complicated that the Javanese had been unable to put it out, and had sent for this special crew from Texas. Even then it had taken special equipment, three months of hard work, and thirty million dollars to extinguish the blaze! It's no wonder that oil companies are so careful about sparks among the oil derricks. Isn't it amazing that Asher's shoes just happen to be made of *"iron"* and *"brass"*, the same metal combination we see used in oil derricks today?

The Fountain of Jacob

Deuteronomy 33:28 explains to us that:

Israel then shall dwell in safety alone: the fountain of Jacob shall be upon a land of corn and wine; also his heavens shall drop down dew.

This verse tells us three things that can be of help to us in our treasure hunt. The first partial sentence declares: *"Israel then shall dwell in safety alone."* The *"then"*, I imagine, speaks of the time that the treasure is found and the oil discovered. The phrase *"...in safety alone"* tells us that she will have no allies ready to protect her, yet she will be safe. This condition squares with Ezekiel 38. Israel's defense, her safety, is, as Ezekiel 38 so dramatically describes, only the Lord God. The next phrase in Deuteronomy 33:28 is *"...the fountain of Jacob."* What is the fountain of Jacob? Is it the same as Joseph's well (many versions say *"fountain"*) in Genesis 49:22? The answer, I believe, is yes! Jacob's fountain and Joseph's well are one and the same for the following reasons.

> (1) In Genesis 49 after Joseph's well is mentioned as part of the patriarchal blessing, verse 26 informs us that *"The blessings of thy father have prevailed above the blessings of my progenitors...they shall be on the head of Joseph, and on the crown of the head of him..."* The *"blessings"* of Jacob are to be found on the head of Joseph!

> (2) Jacob's fountain *"shall be upon a land of corn and wine"* (Deuteronomy 33:28). Joseph's blessings include: *"...Blessed of the Lord be his land..."* (verse 13); *"And for the precious fruits brought forth by the sun..."* (verse 14); *"And for the precious things of the earth and fulness thereof..."* (verse 16). Joseph's land would indeed be *"a land of corn and wine"*.

> (3) Jacob's fountain is to be upon a land where the *"heavens shall drop down dew"* (verse 28). The last of Joseph's blessings in verse 13 include *"...for the dew..."*

We may conclude, then, by biblical evidence, that Joseph's *"well"* and Jacob's *"fountain"* are one and the same.

Is Joseph's Well an Oil Well?

The next question is a little more difficult, and the answer is much more difficult. Yet, it is there, buried deep in the sand of scriptural secrecy.

Is Joseph's *"well"* – Jacob's *"fountain"* - an oil well, or even a great oil field? It is my belief and conclusion that, indeed, the latter is a biblical and physical fact. This *"fountain"* is a great oil field yet to be discovered and developed. I am convinced that God buried this treasure deep in the heart of the *"Promised Land"* when *"He divided unto the nations their inheritance."* This treasure was buried (hidden) and not to be discovered until the *"last days"* (Genesis 49:1). The timely discovery of this rich resource would *"prolong your days in the land"* (Deuteronomy 32:47). It would provide Israel with a powerful position for this perplexing last days period. There would now be an overpowering magnetism in Israel for oil thirsty industrial nations. It is even conceivable that these parched national neighbors might come into Israel's front yard to seek a drink at Joseph well!

CHAPTER 6

Breaking the Code

From the very beginning of our treasure hunt we have looked faithfully through our Bible treasure map for clues that might help us locate the elusive "**X**". After we find the "**X**" we will know where to dig. Meticulously we have searched out and listed each clue. Integrated with the clues were hidden meanings and cryptic symbols. As almost every clue referred to the land in some way, we concluded that the land was to be a key for our search. Then we made a most important discovery: There was a cipher, a code woven in amongst the clues. We called it the anatomy code, for it utilized parts of the human body to symbolize or stand for location. Let us briefly recap the code discovery. Joseph's head appeared first. The *"blessings"* were to be found on the *head* of Joseph, yea even upon his crown. Then Joseph's younger brother Benjamin enters the code. It was promised Benjamin that he would dwell safely *"between his shoulders."* We established that these were Joseph's shoulders. Then we came upon the strange passage that spoke of Gad *"tearing"* his arm with the *"crown of the head."* When we got the last anatomy code clue our imaginations just exploded. Asher was going to *"dip his foot in oil!"* He was going to have shoes made of brass and iron! We knew then that the anatomy code was indeed hiding a great oil discovery. We were sure that if we could break the code, we could find the oil! So, let's break it!

We know that the Promised Land and the anatomy code go hand in hand. They must! The context of scripture won't allow us to believe anything else. The code unlocks the secret that the land has held for millennia. Let's go together to the land.

We Find Joseph's Head

First of all we must locate the head of Joseph in the Promised Land. Remember that Joseph's name won't be attached to any tribal land in Canaan, but the land coming to Joseph would actually be a double portion. It now seems rather simple, doesn't it? If we cross over Jordan and find the tribal lands of Ephraim and Manasseh we will surely discover Joseph's head! Let's look now at map #1. This map shows us the Promised Land. It also demarcates the land of each tribe. Notice how different each portion is from each of the others. It is apparent that the reason for the dividing of the land was not democratic or politically *"fair"*. The *"straight line method"* used to divide states such as Colorado, Wyoming, and North and South Dakota was not used. When you first took at the tribal distribution of land you wonder if anybody was responsible for planning who would settle where. Some tribes have large land holdings, while others are quite small. This is the view of the natural eye, the conclusion of the natural mind. But the division of the land into tribal units was not a natural project; it was a supernatural project. It was God, not man.

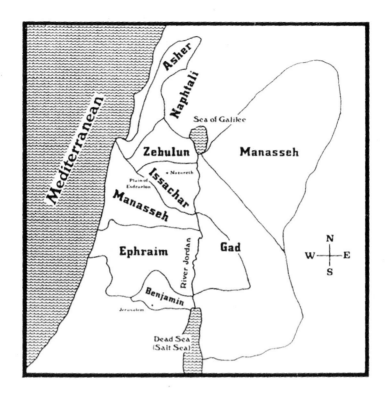

Map 1

The Profile of Joseph's Head

Now look at map #2. This is the same as map #1 except the lands of Ephraim and Manasseh have been boldly outlined that they might stand out from their neighbors. Look at the map closely. Do you see it? Do you see Joseph's head? Imagine yourself standing behind Joseph. You are looking at his back. Joseph's head is turned to his left so that you can see a *profile* of his head. He is looking at the Mediterranean Sea. Do you see the crown on his head? Notice the Jordan River. It forms the back of Joseph head. There are two divisions as Manasseh forms the crown and Ephraim forms the head. Notice the classical styling of the nose as it follows the Mediterranean coastline. Follow on around as the line of the nose turns east, or right, to make the mouth and then the chin. Right here is a good place to say, *"Wow Jim, that sure looks like a head with a crown on it, but could it possibly be?"*

Map 2

Joseph's Shoulders

Let's see if we can confirm the conclusion that this is indeed Joseph head, and not a figment of our imagination. Do you remember the scripture concerning Benjamin? It is Deuteronomy 33:12, *"And of Benjamin he said, the beloved of the Lord...shall dwell between his shoulders"*. We established that *"his shoulders"* were Joseph's shoulders.

Look now at map #3. Do you see the tribe of Benjamin? Benjamin is dwelling between Joseph's shoulders!

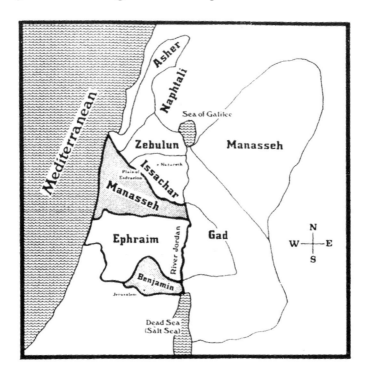

Map 3

This is solid proof that the lines on the map that look like Joseph's head are in fact Joseph's head, for Benjamin is there exactly situated between Joseph's shoulders! Isn't our God amazing?

Now let us look closely at map #4. This map shows the tribe of Zebulun and Issachar outlined so that we see them clearly. Do you see where they are? They are situated side by side, but more importantly, they are both located on Joseph head!

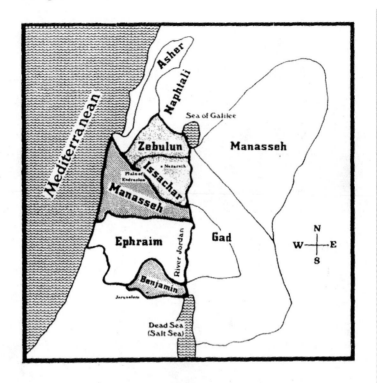

Map 4

From the very beginning we established that the *"blessing"*, the great oil discovery must be <u>on</u> Joseph's head. God had actually anointed his head with oil. Therefore any tribe, such as Zebulun or Issachar that has oil must be located on Joseph's head. These two tribes according to Deuteronomy 33:19, " *...shall suck of the abundance of the seas, and of treasures hid in the sand."* Looking at the map we can see that Zebulun only touches the Sea of Galilee, and Issachar doesn't border on any sea. Question - How can these two tribal lands provide *"the abundance of the seas"* if they aren't next to *"seas"*? The answer is easier than the question. If what is being sucked out of Zebulun and Issachar is oil, then the pool of oil is so big that it is *"couched"* beneath both the Sea of Galilee and the Mediterranean Sea! What a gigantic oil discovery that would be! Everything is fitting fine so far, isn't it?

Gad's Torn Arm

The tribe of Gad now draws our attention. Gad is not an oil-producing tribe, but Gad is useful in helping us with the anatomy code, as well as providing the position of Joseph's head. Map #5 gives us the bold outline of Gad's territory. Notice that it is on the east side of the Jordan River. Actually two and a half tribes held territory on the east of Jordan. Manasseh, because of her size, was given land on both sides of the Jordan. So then, we say that half of Manasseh's tribe is on each side of the river. Reuben and Gad were located entirely on the east side.

Looking at map #5, observe that Gad has a long section of land that proceeds north following up the line of the Jordan River. This *"arm"* of land is *"torn"* by the jagged line of the Jordan. The crown of the head of Joseph actually tears the line of the arm of Gad's land. Let's take another look at Deuteronomy 33:20: *"And of Gad he said, Blessed be he that enlargeth Gad: he dwelleth as a lion, and teareth the arm with the crown of the head"*. The second phrase of the verse *"...Blessed be he that enlargeth Gad"* is speaking of Manasseh, for it is through Manasseh's natural land flow that the arm of Gad's land is extended (enlarged).

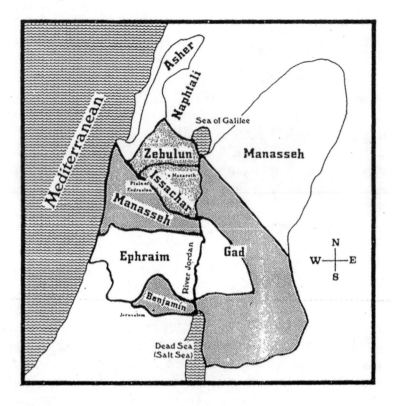

Map 5

Manasseh, of course, is the *"crown of the head"* that *"teareth the arm"* of Gad's tribal territory. Isn't that something special? The anatomy code is even helpful to us in a secondary support!

Asher Dips His Foot in Oil!

And now for the really big one! Let's zero in on the tribe of Asher. Deuteronomy 33:24 says, *"And of Asher he said, Let Asher be blessed with children; let him be acceptable to his brethren, and <u>let him dip his foot in oil</u>."*

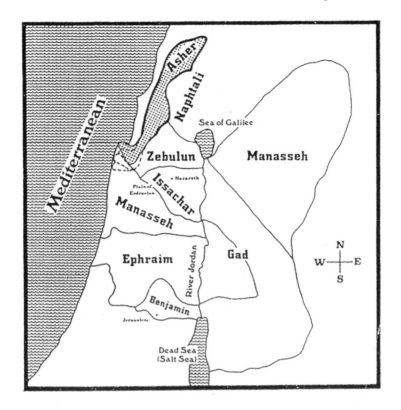

Map 6

Map 6 shows us the borders of Asher's land. As you look at it do you see that the land is shaped like a long leg? The top of the leg is north and the contour moves from north to south. The front of the leg faces the Mediterranean Sea to the west, while the back or calf of the leg borders Naphtali and Zebulun. Isn't it just too amazing that Asher's foot, which is to be dipped in oil, is on the *"head of Joseph, yea and on the crown of the head of him who was separate from his brethren?"* (Genesis 49:26)

How much oil will Asher be dipping his foot into? It has to be an enormous field of petroleum, for the oil derricks will be so close that an airplane flight over Asher's foot would give the impression that he was wearing a shoe made of iron and brass (Deuteronomy 33:25). What a dramatic and eloquent picture! The portion of land that looks like a foot, which is connected to the portion of land that looks like a leg, will dip into a pool of oil so enormous that it is beyond our imaginings. The foot will wear a shoe made of non-shoe material, iron and brass! Wow! Genesis 49:20 will be fulfilled abundantly: *"Out of Asher his bread shall be fat..."* The word for fat in this verse is easily translated *"oil"*.

About Maps

Look in the back of almost any Bible or in any Bible Atlas and you'll find a map of the ancient territories of the twelve tribes of Israel similar to the maps in this chapter. One thing you will notice is that the borders between the tribes (if there are any borders at all) are not exactly the same as the borders on the maps in this chapter. In fact, if you compare maps between Bibles and Atlases, you'll find that none of the tribal borders on any of the maps are exactly the same. The reason for this apparent discrepancy is that historical territorial information for the era is not exacting and sometimes one piece of historical data contradicts another. For example one historic record may place an ancient city in a specific location and another may place the same city in a different location. Placement of exact borders on a map of ancient Israel often is at the discretion and historical interpretation of the map's cartographer. Don't be too alarmed if the map in your Bible shows Joseph's crown riding lower on his brow, or if Asher's foot is turned to the left instead of the right. Every map agrees with the general geographic location and shape of the tribal boundaries. Considering the thousands of years that have transpired since the children of Israel entered into Canaan and the land's continual history of conquest, destruction and change, this agreement of geographic location and configuration provides overwhelming evidence of the anthropomorphic connection of the land to the scriptures.

CHAPTER 7

A "P.S." on Jacob's Blessing

We have discussed at great length the blessing that Jacob gave to his sons as he lay dying in Egypt. Our focus has been on the part of the blessing that had to do with oil and its discovery. There is another piece of information concerning Jacob's blessing that fits in very nicely with our study. Let me share it with you. Turn your mind biblically back to the time and place where Jacob himself received the *"blessing"* from his father Isaac. The account is found in the twenty-seventh chapter of Genesis. Isaac was old and he was anticipating his death. He asked his oldest son, Esau to come in to him that he might ask of him a special request. Isaac wanted to taste fresh venison again before he died. Esau, the man of the field, was a great hunter, and he hastened to the hunt to do his father's bidding. While Esau was gone, Jacob, having been informed of the situation by his mother, impersonated Esau and tricked his father into giving *him* the blessing (Jacob had already bartered Esau out of his birthright!).

Birthright and Blessing were, by tradition connected to the firstborn son. The birthright of the firstborn included a double portion of the father's estate, including the responsibility to care for any unwed daughters and the widow or widows of the deceased. Essentially, the firstborn son took over as head of the family and the family's possessions. The blessing was also, by tradition given to the firstborn son.

The blessing was more of a spiritual inheritance, passed down from father to son. The blessing dealt more with sacred relationships and the promise of *"good things to come."* The right of the firstborn son to these benefits wasn't guaranteed. They could be traded (as with Esau and his birthright for a bowl of soup), given up voluntarily, by deception (as with Jacob and his father's blessing) or taken away at the discretion of God or of the patriarch (as with Ishmael and Isaac). The blessing not going to the firstborn, however, was outside of tradition and a rare occurrence. The fact that it happened in four consecutive generations (Isaac, Jacob, Joseph, and Ephraim) must mean that God's hand and sovereignty were at work to enact some plan beyond the scope of these men and their traditions.

"The Fatness of the Earth"

The first part of Isaac's blessing that he unknowingly gave to Jacob is the center of our attention. It is found in Genesis 27:28: *"Therefore God give thee of the dew of heaven, and <u>the fatness of the earth</u>..."* In the Hebrew this literally means *"the oil of the ground"*! Isn't that intriguing? But we are not through with this part of our story yet! Esau comes back from the hunt to give his father the fresh venison and finds out that Jacob has bested him again. Verse thirty-four says: *"And when Esau heard the word of his father* (that Jacob had tricked him and the blessing would stand*), he cried with a great and exceeding bitter cry, and said unto his father, Bless me, even me also, 0 my father."* Esau continued to weep bitterly before his father, asking him if there wasn't some kind of blessing that Isaac might yet give him. Verse thirty-nine gives us Isaac's answer: *"...Behold, thy <u>dwelling</u>*

shall be the fatness of the earth... " (the oil of the ground). Isaac uses the same phrase, *"the fatness of the earth"*, both in Jacob's and in Esau's blessing. What does this show us about these two men, and more importantly, about the nations formed out of them? Let's look at Esau first. Esau was renamed Edom because of his redness (Genesis 25:25-30). As you look at the map of the Middle East during the time of the dividing of the twelve tribes, you can see Edom (also Idumea) as a territory beginning at the Dead Sea and extending south in a fan shape. It was to be known as Arabia. Today Edom (Esau) is Arabia. Isaac's blessing to Esau has been fulfilled for Esau is indeed *"dwelling"* on *"the fatness* (oil) *of the earth"*. Who has more oil (fatness) than Arabia? At this writing the world must answer *"nobody"*. But praise God, we know differently! Jacob has more oil, a lot more oil, and one day the world will know it to the greater glory of God.

Saudi Arabia, as of 2003 had 261.7 billion barrels of proven oil reserves. Esau's children, the Saudis, produce about 9.95 million barrels of oil per day.

A note for you geology buffs: The Dead Sea is at the bottom of the earth rift (tear) that comes up through the Sinai. Tectonic forces could have actually squeezed the oil, like squeezing a toothpaste tube, down into Arabia. Wouldn't it be something if a latter-day earthquake in Arabia forced the oil (toothpaste) up the Jordan River (tube) fault line? It could go all the way up to the top of Joseph's head.

Let's Recap

Let us now briefly sum up to see *"what"* we have found, and *where* it is found. Jacob and Moses teamed up to bless the children of Israel with blessings that would help fulfill God's covenant with Abraham. The blessings were to be realized _after_ Israel had possessed the land and divided it up into prescribed tribal territories. Some of the blessings were to be received a _long time_ after the demarcation of the land (Genesis 49:1). These *"last days"* that Jacob spoke of in Genesis 49:1 are the very days that we are living in now. We are now, and will be later, the eyewitnesses of the fulfillment of God's covenant with Abraham. This is especially important to born-again Christians who are in truth the *"seed"* of Abraham, and *"heirs according to the promise."* (Galatians 3:29)

When Will This Oil Be Found?

As I write these words, I know two things concerning this question. The first thing I know is that oil _has not_ been discovered yet. The second thing I know is that oil _will be_ discovered sometime in the years to come. The discovery could be at any time. It is no secret that the modern state of Israel desperately needs Jacob's blessing right now. Her oil dependency on other nations makes her vulnerable both economically and militarily. With the international power blocs saying "no" to her oil needs, and a national inflation rate that is unmanageable, how many more years could it be?

Since the words above were originally penned in 1981 a great deal has changed but the overall situation remains much the same. Twenty-four years of oil exploration, geological testing, and prayer have transpired. As we will see in Book II, many explorers searching for Israel's treasure have come and gone. The geological proof is in, the first back bays of an oil sea have been tapped; today we are witnessing the beginning of this prophecy's fulfillment. Israel needs oil independence and the safety of autonomy more than ever. The message has more relevance today than ever before.

CHAPTER 8

Gog and Magog

When the great oil fields that anoint Joseph's head *are* discovered, and the neighboring nations recognize the impact of the discovery, what will they say? What will they do? As far as the Arab nations are concerned, it won't make much difference what they say or do, as they are extremely bellicose anyway. However, there are other nations in that part of the world that would be extremely interested in a new oil field discovery. The Russian bear, a near neighbor of Israel, is foraging even now for new *"earth honey"* in which to dip its hungry paw. The bear must feed her brood that guards her European hunting grounds. She hungers for *"honey"* and thirsts for blood.

The Hooks in the Jaws

Ezekiel thirty-eight begins with:

And the word of the Lord came unto me, saying,

Son of man, set thy face against Gog, the land of Magog, the chief prince of Meschech and Tubal, and prophesy against him.

And say, Thus saith the Lord God; Behold, I am against thee, 0 Gog, the chief prince of Meshech and Tubal:

The line is drawn quickly and forcefully. God is setting himself against Gog and Magog! There is no doubt about the identification of Gog. It is Russia. If you happen to be using an ASV, NASB or a Jerusalem Bible translation instead of the King James Version, you will see the word *"Rosh"* used in place of *"Gog"*. Magog speaks of some of the tribes or sub-nations that have evolved from and with the chief prince of Meshech (Moscow) and Tubal (Tobolsk). Russia is a conglomerate of these sub-nations. Their original springing forth can be traced all the way back to Genesis 10:2. This verse gives us the Sons of Japheth, who was a son of Noah. They are listed as: *"The sons of Japheth, Gomer and Magog, and Madai, and Javan, and Tubal, and Meschech, and Tiras."*

> *"The Jewish tradition of Gog and Magog is quite distinct from the Bible and describes 70 national angels, some of which have fallen and others are still with God. The Biblical prophecy says that Gog – who in the tradition is the angel of the nation called Magog – will be defeated after he leads an army to attack Israel from the four corners of the land. This angel therefore represents the spirit of anti-Semitism."*
>
> Wikipedia

So, Russia and God will be literally at sword point. Ezekiel thirty-eight, verse three says: *"...I am against thee, 0 Gog."* We know that Russia has been *"against"* God since 1917 and the communist revolution. The great confrontation will finally take place even as these verses go on to describe it:

> *And I will turn thee back, and put hooks into thy jaws, and I will bring thee forth, and all thine army, horses and horsemen, all of them clothed with all sorts of armor, even a great*

company with bucklers and shields, all of them handling swords:

Persia, Ethiopia, and Libya with them; all of them with shield and helmet:

Ezekiel 38:4-5

Verse four tells us that God *Himself* is going to bring about this great confrontation. *"I will...put hooks into thy jaws, and I will bring thee forth..."* The Russian bear will have *"hooks"* put into her jaws that she may be drawn southward into Israel. What do you think these *"hooks"* will be? The word *"hooks"* is most certainly symbolic of something that has a drawing effect on Russia to bring her into this mighty confrontation. Do you think possibly that this *"hook in the jaw"* could be the newly-discovered oil fields of Israel?

It is Only a Matter of Time

Computer workups tell us that the Russian republics are in a state of diminishing returns. Part of this is attributable to the breaking up of the USSR into independent and separate smaller republics. Oil reserves are lower and have been kidnapped by inter-republic competition. If this scenario is correct, then it would seem feasible to think that Russia and some of her allies might consider the new oil fields an irresistible drawing attraction.

As of 2003 Russia's *"explored reserves"* were at 58.8 billion barrels. Her current daily production is about 11.6 million barrels per day. If she keeps production in pace with the current rate of increase in demand, Russia's reserves will be depleted by 2020.

We see three of her allies in verse five. They are Persia (Iran), Ethiopia, and Libya. At this writing Iran has not aligned herself with Russia, but it is only a matter of time before she does. Since the tragic American hostage situation, Iran has little political or economic involvement with the United States in particular, or the West in general. Having been semi-industrialized and semi-modernized by the late Shah Pahlavi, she must ally herself with someone who can supply her with the industrial and military material to keep on going. Where she was almost completely supplied by the United States, she must now look for another *"complete"* supplier. Russia is the only viable candidate who stands ready to do that. So, as I said, it is only a matter of time.

> *"Russia and Iran signed a deal Sunday that would deliver nuclear fuel to the Middle East country for the startup of its first reactor — a project the United States had for years pushed Moscow to drop, claiming Iran is trying to build a nuclear bomb."*
>
> Associated Press February 27, 2005

Ethiopia is a Russian satellite state. For many years Ethiopia was pro-Western, but Soviet saturation has now set in.

> **Addis Ababa, December 12, 2002 (ENA) -** Ethiopia and Russia have signed a diplomatic and service passport free visa agreement. Ambassador Lipnyakov on his part said the agreement would be instrumental in further strengthening the cooperation between Ethiopia and Russia.

Libya is a country large in land, small in people, poor in agriculture and industry, and rich in oil. Libya has come under Russian influence also. In 1974, Russia brought pressure to bear upon Colonel Moamar Gaddafi, the Libyan leader, to expel the Americans from their bases in Libya, charging them with being imperialists. As soon as the American *"imperialists"* moved out of the Libyan bases, the Russian imperialists moved in! That was in 1974. In 1978, Russian and Cuban troops helped the *"revolutionary army"* bring Ethiopia in line with Russian communism. It was in 1979 that the American hostages were taken captive in Iran. They were released in 1981. The dates sort of move along together as if someone or something is orchestrating a concert for conflict.

Russia Hopes To Supply Libya With MiG-31 Jets

MOSCOW, Jul 8, 1999 -- Russia hopes to supply Libya with a number of MiG-31 interceptor jets, the head of a Russian aircraft manufacturer was quoted as saying on Wednesday. The MiG-31 Foxhound, a long-range interceptor able to operate with or without ground system support, has been the mainstay of Russian air defense.

Reuters, 07-08-99

The Last Days

Isn't it amazing how a biblical prophecy given in the sixth century before the birth of Christ demonstrates such definitive accuracy twenty centuries after his birth? It is a graphic demonstration for us that these are the *"last days"*, or as Ezekiel says, *"the latter years"*. I could not have written these words thirty-five years ago with any suggestion that these three countries would be in Russia's camp, for at that time there was not even a hint that they ever would be! Look at the years together:

- 1973 - Yom Kippur War and oil embargo

- ☐ 1974 - Libya goes Russian

- ☐ Ethiopia follows in 1978

- ☐ 1979-81 Iran moved toward the hammer and sickle

Just think of it!

On the surface, Russian-Israeli relations have warmed. Israel currently buys 80% of its foreign oil from Russia. If Israel were to quit Russia as a major oil customer overnight, the relationship would immediately cool. But beneath the surface the Russian alliance with Persian Gulf and North African nations has matured into a mutual self-help pact. Russia supplies the PLO and Persian Gulf countries with arms and war materiel. The Arab nations provide much needed cash to Russia.

Yet these three nations are not the only allies of Russia that will move against Israel's *"unwalled villages"*. Ezekiel 38:6 declares that *"Gomer, and all his bands; the house of Togarmah of the north quarters, and all his band,"* will also be included in this great military campaign. Gomer is the ancient name for Germany, while Togarmah is the ancient name for Turkey. East Germany, of course, had been Soviet-dominated since 1945. West and East Germany are now joined as one and will move in as a national unit - just as the singular name *"Gomer"* implies. There is no East Gomer and West Gomer!

Germany, Russia mull U.S. missile shield

January 30, 2001

MOSCOW, Russia -- Objections to the United States' new missile defence programme have topped the agenda in talks between German and Russian military officials...Colonel-General Valery Manilov, Russia's First Deputy Chief of Staff, said an alternative Russian system involving NATO and the European Union would leave the military balance untouched and serve the same purpose of eliminating the threat of missile strikes by *"so-called rogue regimes."*

CNN.com

Turkey, like Iran, is situated on Russia's southern border, and will give way to her pressure.

Turkey-Russia relations

Given their dynamically growing economic co-operation, the leaders of Turkey and Russia are now working for closer political dialogue to match.

For centuries, Turkey and Russia have been rivals for regional supremacy. Recently, the two countries have realised that friendly relations are in the interest of them both. Accordingly, co-operation rather than rivalry appears to dominate their ties. This development has been welcome by the EU, which sees these countries as the two largest imponderables on the European horizon.

Euractive.com May 2, 2005

What is the Timetable?

When will all this happen? When we consider the frequency of these recent dates, it appears as if it could be soon. Ezekiel 38:8 declares:

> *After many days thou shalt be visited: in the latter years thou shalt come into the land that is brought back from the sword; and is gathered out of many people, against the mountains of Israel, which have been always waste: but it is brought forth out of the nations, and they shall dwell safely all of them.*

What an informative verse! It gives us five hints as to when this huge military machine is to move into Israel. First, it will be *"after many days."* The prophetic day is a year, and so it reads more correctly *"after many years."* This has already happened; many years have passed. Second, it is to be *"in the latter years."* If we study Matthew twenty-four to give us the *"signs of the times,"* we may conclude that we are now in the *"latter years."* Third, Russia and her allies are to come into a *"land that is brought back from the sword!"* Fourth, the nation is to be *"gathered out of many people."* Israel, today, is exactly that: She is a new nation literally *"gathered out of many people."* Fifth, the enemy from the north is to descend upon the *"mountains of Israel, which have been always waste..."* This waste land was a result of the *"seven times"* judgment spoken of in Leviticus 26:27-45. Verse thirty-three sums it up briefly:

> *And I will scatter you among the heathen, and will draw out a sword after you: and your land shall be desolate, and your cities waste.*

Israel's wasteland was a direct result of God's judgment.

The Wastes Shall Be Builded

On the other hand, God promised that he would reverse the process when he restored Israel. Ezekiel 36:6-11 is the declaration of this promise:

> *Prophesy therefore concerning the land of Israel, and say unto the mountains, and to the hills, to the rivers, and to the valleys, Thus saith the Lord God; Behold, I have spoken in my jealousy and in my fury, because ye have borne the shame of the heathen:*
>
> *Therefore thus saith the Lord God; I have lifted up mine hand, Surely the heathen that are about you, they shall bear their shame.*
>
> *But ye, 0 mountains of Israel, ye shall shoot forth your branches, and yield your fruit to my people of Israel; for they are at hand to come.*
>
> *For, behold, I am for you, and I will turn unto you, and ye shall be tilled and sown:*
>
> *And I will multiply men upon you, all the house of Israel, even all of it: and the cities shall be inhabited, and the wastes shall be builded:*
>
> *And I will multiply upon you man and beast; and they shall increase and bring fruit: and I will settle you after your old estates, and will do better unto you than at your beginnings: and ye. shall know that I am the Lord.*

Israel today is an agricultural wonder. Land that was desert thirty years ago thrives today with incredibly diverse agricultural products managed under the world's most advanced horticultural systems. No other country matches the intensity and diversity of Israel's agricultural output.

"Thou Shalt Think an Evil Thought"

The five things that we have just mentioned are not in a future time frame. These conditions and situations already exist. The only thing that speaks of the future in Ezekiel 38:8 is the first sentence, *"After many days thou shalt be visited: in the latter years..."* This refers to *"Gog and Magog"* being *"visited"* by the Lord God and drawn down into Israel toward Judgment. The next three verses, nine through eleven, describe the power and the malice of Gog:

> 9. *Thou shalt ascend and come like a storm, thou shalt be like a cloud to cover the land...*

> 10. *...at the same time shall things come into thy mind, and thou shalt think an evil thought:*

> 11. *And thou shalt say, I will go up to the land of unwalled villages...to them that are at rest, that dwell safely... without walls... neither bars nor gates...*

What is Gog's thinking at this point? What evil thought has come into his mind? Ezekiel 38:12 has the answer:

To take a spoil, and to take a prey; to turn thine hand upon the desolate places that are now inhabited, and upon the people that are gathered out of the nations, which have gotten cattle and goods, that dwell in the midst of the land.

Look at the first four words of verse twelve: *"To take a spoil..."* Is it coincidental that the last three letters of *"spoil"* spell *"oil"*? It may or may not be prophetic, but it is interesting, isn't it? It is inconceivable that this great invasion force would risk international repercussions for just *"cattle and goods"*. Verse thirteen speaks of gold and silver, but this can't stand by itself either. If Gog was chiefly interested in cattle and goods, and silver and gold, then the attack would have to be directed against another country. Israel is not even moderately wealthy in these liquid assets. It would be like Little Red Riding Hood's wolf invading Mother Hubbard's cupboard. But what if...? What if there is an enormous oil discovery *"in the midst of the land?"* Now that is a reason for an invasion of this magnitude! This would answer some of the questions that have arisen. Why would a community of nations as obviously gigantic as Russia need allies to invade a country as tiny as Israel? Why attack at this particular time? Why not use nuclear weapons instead of conventional weaponry?

At this moment we can only speculate what the *"evil thought"* of Gog's really is, that is, what the motivation behind it is to be. However, it is no secret what the heavenly reason is. It is disclosed in the sixteenth verse:

And thou shalt come up against my people of Israel, as a cloud to cover the land; it shall be in the latter days, and I will bring thee against my land, that the heathen may know me, when I shall be sanctified in thee, 0 Gog, before their eyes.

> *"So, let's add things up, shall we? An Israeli oil strike would bring down the wrath of the Islamic world, threaten Russia's plans to use its own oil as a future strategic weapon, and earn Israel a new favored status among the Europeans, bringing all the players in Ezekiel's Gog-Magog invasion to center stage at the same time."*
>
> Jack Kinsella

The World Sees God's Holiness

The Lord God Jehovah is going to be sanctified before the entire world. Gog represents internationally-organized evil, and his defeat will represent the defeat of this internationally-organized evil.

The remainder of Ezekiel thirty describes the wrath and judgment of God on Gog and the allied invasion force. God uses both natural and supernatural weapons against Gog. The slaughter is indescribable. Blood colors the mountains and covers the plain. Destruction is utter. *"Defeat"* can not describe the situation. Only one-sixth of the invasion force survives to limp home and testify to the power of Israel's God.

CHAPTER 9

What About Armageddon?

As awful as the battle and destruction between Gog and God is, it is not the battle called Armageddon. Some feel that the battle of Gog is the first battle between God and the national world systems in the latter years. Ezekiel 39:9 teaches that the weapons left on the battlefield by Gog's defeated armies will require seven years to burn. This figure offers speculation that the Gog invasion is the trigger for the seven-year tribulatory period spoken of by Daniel and John. Whether this is true or not remains to be seen, but the time of Armageddon's horror is fixed.

Revelation 16:16 tells us of this dramatic and apocalyptic battlefield. The word *"Armageddon"* means the *"Mountain of Megiddo"*. In Old Testament times there was a city of Megiddo located on the *"great plain"*, or plain of Megiddo. This historic battleground is located between the Galilean hills and the mountains of Israel. It was here that Barak defeated the Canaanites, and Gideon the Midianites. The battle of Armageddon is really more of a war than a battle.

> *"Throughout history Megiddo and the Jezreel Valley have been Ground Zero for battles that determined the very course of civilization. It is no wonder that the author of Revelation believed Armageddon, the penultimate battle between good and evil, would also take place in this region!"*
>
> **The Battles of Armageddon**, Eric H. Cline

Not only will soldiers be gathered at Megiddo, but also in the south and central parts of the Holy Land. God declares that His sword *"shall be bathed in heaven: behold it shall come down upon Idumea (Edom)..."* (Isaiah 34:5). Edom is in the south. Joel 3:2 tells us that it is in the valley of Jehoshaphat that God will gather the nations and plead for his people. Some experts feel that the valley of Jehoshaphat is in central Palestine somewhere between Jerusalem and the Jordan River. Revelation 14:20 says:

> *And the winepress was trodden without the city, and blood came out of the winepress, even unto the horse bridles, by the space of a thousand and six hundred furlongs.*

The blood will be five feet deep for the length of 200 miles! That is the approximate length of Israel today. This war of Armageddon will cover the entire land. Who is it that will be fighting in this terrible war?

Power Blocs of Nations

The Bible tells us that there are international power blocs, or groups of countries that will come against Israel. There are four of these groups, or power blocs, and they come from each direction of the compass.

The northern group contains Russia and her selected allies that we have already discussed in the context of Ezekiel 38. It appears that this battle begins the tribulation period. Although the Russian invasion seems to be part and parcel with this furious flurry of end-time battles, it is also treated separately in scripture.

Daniel chapter 2 tells us of the western confederacy that will move against Israel. It is a group of countries that will represent the old Roman Empire. Daniel, interpreting King Nebuchadnezzar's dream, calls this power bloc *"the fourth kingdom."* Daniel himself has a dream that is described for us in the seventh chapter of Daniel. It expands Nebuchadnezzar's dream. Daniel 7:7 explains:

> *After this I saw in the night visions, and behold a fourth beast, dreadful and terrible, and strong exceedingly; and it had great iron teeth: it devoured and brake in pieces, and stamped the residue with the feet of it: and it was diverse from all the beasts that were before it; and it had ten horns.*

The interpretation of this part of the dream is given in Daniel 7:23, 24:

> *23. Thus he said, the fourth beast shall be the fourth kingdom upon earth, which shall be diverse from all kingdoms, and shall devour the whole earth, and shall tread it down, and break it in pieces.*
>
> *24. And the ten horns out of this kingdom are ten kings that shall arise: and another shall rise after them..."*

The Revived Roman Empire

As we noted, the fourth kingdom was the old Roman Empire, but the ten kings are ten countries that came *"out of the kingdom."* This *"revived"* Roman Empire is the power bloc that will come from the west.

There are those today who believe that this ten nation federation comes out of the European Common Market. The Common Market had its beginning on January 1, 1958, with the six countries of West Germany, Belgium, France, Italy, Holland and Luxembourg as charter members. The three nations of Great Britain, Ireland and Denmark were added on January 1, 1973. The tenth nation, Greece, was officially received into active membership on January 1, 1981. However, the number of members is still in ebb and flow.

The European Common Market evolved in 1992 into the European Union. Today the E.U. includes 28 member countries. In addition to the ten countries above, Austria, Bulgaria, Cyprus, Czech Republic, Estonia, Finland, Hungary, Iceland, Latvia, Lithuania, Malta, Norway, Poland, Portugal, Slovakia, Slovenia, Spain and Turkey are EU members today.

Is the stage now set for the ten horns to fulfill prophecy? The Bible; teaches that three of these horns will be subdued by another who rises *"after"*. He will proceed to take leadership of the entire confederacy, and then move against the most High God. He will *"speak great words against the most High, and shall wear out the saints of the most High..."* (Daniel 7:25) Could the Common Market develop into this?

Yes, of course it could. There are those in Europe who have been looking for a superman kind of leader for years. Henri Spaak, an early Common Market leader, stated it graphically, perhaps prophetically. He announced:

> *We do not want another committee, we have too many already. What we want is a man of sufficient stature to hold the allegiance of all people, and to lift us out of the economic morass into which we are sinking. Send us such a man and be he god or devil, we will receive him!*

As far a Biblical prophecy is concerned, don't worry too much about the EU now including more than ten countries, disqualifying it from being the *"ten kings"* mentioned in Daniel. The original ten countries are the only full members of the EU. The other "newcomers" are relegated to *"Associate"* or *"Observer"* roles.

The Kings of the South and East

The *"king of the south"* heads the southern power bloc. Egypt is the leader, but there will undoubtedly be Arab countries in close alliance with her. Egypt, although oil poor, has been historically the leader of the Arab countries.

The Arab Persian Gulf and North African Muslim nations have become radically anti-West (U.S.) and have always been radically anti-Israel. Egypt, playing the role of moderate since Camp David and the return of the Sinai no longer speaks to the sentiments of the Muslim nations.

The fourth and last power bloc is what the Bible refers to as the *"kings of the east"*. We can't say much about this, for the scripture only mentions it twice (Daniel 11:44 and Revelation 16:12). However, it seems that they must represent China, India and Japan, as well as other minor states.

Asia, including China, India, and Korea, is the largest emerging market the world has ever seen. As it grows into maturity, its appetites and power will be capable of eclipsing every other national group on the planet.

The Whole Earth Is Against Zion!

It seems as if all four corners of the earth have been armed and are marching toward Zion! They come to represent by force their own economic interests. They come to do battle against any adversary that would keep them from their quest, their goal. They are prepared to do battle against each other, but then something turns their fury toward God and His people.

Christ's Triumphant Return

This is the time of the Lord's triumphant return in power and great glory. The military might of the world is aligned against him. The Beast and the False Prophet await the calamity of the coming Christ. John describes it in Revelation 19:11 – 21:

> *And I saw heaven opened, and behold a white horse; and he that sat upon him was called Faithful and True, and in righteousness he doth judge and make war.*
>
> *His eyes were as a flame of fire, and on his head were many crowns; and he had a name written, that no man knew, but he himself.*
>
> *And he was clothed with a vesture dipped in blood: and his name is called The Word of God.*
>
> *And the armies which were in heaven followed him upon white horses, clothed in fine linen, white and clean.*
>
> *And out of his mouth goeth a sharp sword, that with it he should smite the nations: and he shall rule them with a rod of iron: and he*

treadeth the winepress of the fierceness and wrath of Almighty God.

And he hath on his vesture and on his thigh a name written, KING OF KINGS, AND LORD OF LORDS.

And I saw an angel standing in the sun; and he cried with a loud voice, saying, to all the fowls that fly in the midst of heaven, Come and gather yourselves together unto the supper of the great God;

That ye may eat the flesh of kings, and the flesh of captains, and the flesh of mighty men, and the flesh of horses, and of them that sit on them, and the flesh of all men, both free and bond, both small and great.

And I saw the beast, and the kings of the earth, and their armies, gathered together to make war against him that sat on the horse, and against his army.

And the beast was taken, and with him the false prophet that wrought miracles before him, with which he deceived them that had received the mark of the beast, and them that worshipped his image. These both were cast alive into a lake of fire burning with brimstone.

And the remnant were slain with the sword of him that sat upon the horse, which sword proceeded out of his mouth: and all the fowls were filled with their flesh.

CHAPTER 10

Why?

What was it that brought all these armies to this small, rather insignificant section of the earth's crust? For years I wrestled with this question. The battle of Armageddon didn't make sense. Why would the armies of the world be at that place, at that time, for that purpose? It seemed to be the wrong war, at the wrong time, for the wrong reason, at the wrong place. In the natural realm it was. But God - He brings together all things to fulfill his supernatural promises, and involves natural conditions and situations. God knew at the beginning of days, alpha days, what would transpire at the end of days, omega days. He is the alpha and the omega. He is the beginner and the ender.

Alpha is the first letter of the Greek alphabet; Omega is the last. Alpha and Omega symbolize the beginning and the end. Revelation 1:8 states, *"'I am the Alpha and the Omega,' says the Lord God, 'who is, and who was, and who is to come, the Almighty.'"* (NIV)

He is the author and the finisher. He knew. He knew that man would eventually develop a technology that would require a gigantically perverse amount of energy to fuel it. He knew that oil would become the favorite fuel of *"latter day"* nations. He knew that the military and industrial might of each country would be dependent on each country's possession of oil. He knew that during the oil glut of the '50's and '60's man would squander a great portion of that earth honey. He knew that the Arab-Israeli war of 1973 would trigger the energy crisis, the petroleum polarization of the international body politic, and the greatest transfer of wealth in history. He knew that by 1980 all industrial nations would be near hysteria, first for lack of oil, and then for the extortionary price of it. Even though the '80's and '90's would see frantic oil exploration and discovery in the world, the problem had not been abated. Much oil is now being pumped from new non-traditional fields, but I think that this only exacerbates the situation. It serves to have polarized the problems, rather than solved them. The price of petroleum is still very high, and at the first sign of international crisis triggered by terrorism or regional wars, could skyrocket to stratospheric heights. Yet, even this temporary semi-reprieve in supply and demand was foreknown.

We know only too well that the polarization of countries, political factions, economies, and ideologies over oil is far more relevant today than when these words were first penned in 1981. The price of crude oil hit an all time high in 2005.

God Had a Foreknowledge of All Things

The foreknowledge of God about hidden petroleum was just a part of his knowing before. His purposes and subsequent design for natural man's creation and ultimate spiritual relationship was in his mind long before man's earthly kingdom was begun. From man's Edenic beginning he has foundered and fumbled in his half-hearted attempts to add God to his human kingdom. Man rarely realized that God's kingdom was present and operating successfully long before the kingdom of man was born. It was, as we all know, the kingdom of man that was added to the kingdom of God. Coming forth from the mind of God in the extended establishment of his kingdom on earth was a prophetic poem, woven into a scriptural tapestry that will someday hang on the walls of eternity. The temporal and unimportant social designation of *"Jew"* and *"Gentile"* has no place on those eternal walls. They are both appellations by men and for men, used divisively to separate man from man and man from God. In that *"great day coming"* we will have new names *"And the Gentiles shall see thy righteousness, and all kings thy glory: and thou shalt be called by a new name, which the mouth of the Lord shall name."* (Isaiah 62:2) That unity that we have longed for will finally be ours, even as Jesus prayed that it would be:

> *That they all may be one; as thou, Father, art in me, and I in thee, that they also may be one in us: that the world may believe that thou hast sent me.*
>
> *John 17:21*

Temporal Israel is Not Eternal Israel

If the earthly, human designation of *"Jew"* and *"Gentile"* will be subsumed in glory, how about that mighty but mysterious name *"Israel"*? We have already learned that there are seven *"Israels"* that exist biblically and contemporarily.

For a free downloadable copy of Jim Spillman's The Seven Israels go to *www.JimSpillmanMinistries.org*.

Are any of these eternal in nature, or are they all just temporal? It is easily understood that the seventh Israel, the modern state of Israel, even as Germany and England, has no heavenly meaning or place. Israel is an earthly nation couched in earthly history. It is not an entity to be considered in the *"new heaven and the new earth"*:

> *And I saw a new heaven and a new earth: for the first heaven and the first earth were passed away; and there was no more sea.*
>
> *Revelation 21:1*

What of Biblical Israel, of Jacob, the children of Israel coming into Canaan, the Northern Kingdom, and the Babylon returnees? These four Israels are the historic narrative of God's plan to begin the physical counterpart in the presentation of His true, eternal Israel. Again, they were temporal designations standing for the earthly initiation and development of God's redemptive plan. They are not to be exhumed and synthetically restored for life and practice in God's earthly community today. These last days were never meant to be a reprise of the times of the law or practice of the people of the law. Hebrews 7:19 declares: *"For the law made nothing perfect, but the bringing in of a better hope did; by the which we draw nigh unto God."*

The New Israel Relationship

The writer of Hebrews goes on in chapter eight, verses 1 – 13 to discuss their *"new"* Israel relationship in a highly definitive way:

> *Now of the things which we have spoken this is the sum: We have such an high priest, who is set on the right hand of the throne of the Majesty in the heavens;*
>
> *A minister of the sanctuary, and of the true tabernacle, which the Lord pitched, and not man.*

For if he were on earth, he should not be a priest, seeing that there are priests that offer gifts according to the law:

Who serve unto the example and shadow of heavenly things...

But now hath he obtained a more excellent ministry, by how much also he is the mediator of a better covenant, which was established upon better promises.

For if that first covenant had been faultless, then should no place have been sought for the second.

For finding fault with them, he saith, Behold, the days come, saith the Lord, when I will make a new covenant with the house of Israel and with the house of Judah:

Not according to the covenant that I made with their fathers in the day when I took them by the hand to lead them out of the land of Egypt; because they continued not in my covenant, and I regarded them not, saith the Lord.

For this is the covenant that I will make with the house of Israel after those days, saith the Lord; I will put my laws into their mind, and write them in their hearts: and I will be to them a God, and they shall be to me a people:

For I will be merciful to their unrighteousness, and their sins and their iniquities will I remember no more.

In that he saith, A new covenant, he hath made the first old. Now that which decayeth and waxeth old is ready to vanish away.

A Final Word on the Land

This brings us to the consideration of the fifth Israel, the land. Even though the historic, biblical people of Israel lived on the land called *"Canaan"* and then called *"Israel"* this land had a purpose and a place in God's plan that went beyond the history of Bible people. The land was formed, designated and enriched long before Jacob was a prophetic personality. The land came before the people. The land not only has a past, but it has a millennial future. It will play a part in the plan of God until it is replaced by the *"new earth"* (Revelation 21:1).

> Israel will be known as *"the camp of God's people,"* with Jerusalem *"the city he loves"* as its capital (Revelation 20:9) for a thousand years before God's final judgment and the establishment of a *"new earth"*.

The *"Israel of God"*

We must finally remember the *"Israel of God"* of Galatians 6:16. This Israel is the *"household of faith"* established in Christ Jesus. This Israel is the figure of which the other personal Israels were *"shadows"* (Hebrews 8:5). It was conceived in the foreknowledge of God (Romans 8:29), and consummated in the spiritual lives of men (Corinthians 3:16, 17). All of these things that we have studied in this book find their place in the Kingdom of God of which Jesus spoke: *"And I appoint unto you a kingdom, as my Father hath appointed unto me."* (Luke 22:29) The entrance into this kingdom is through the new birth of which Jesus spoke:

> *Jesus answered and said unto him, Verily, verily, I say unto thee, Except a man be born again, he cannot see the kingdom of God.*
>
> *John 3:3*

To learn more about this *"New Birth"* see Appendix A *"Spiritual Help"*

Paul, in Colossians explained it so very well:

Who hath delivered us from the power of darkness, and hath translated us into the kingdom of his dear Son:

In whom we have redemption through his blood, even the forgiveness of sins:

Who is the image of the invisible God, the firstborn of every creature:

For by him were all things created, that are in heaven, and that are in earth, visible and invisible, whether they be thrones, or dominions, or principalities, or powers: all things were created by him, and for him:

And he is before all things, and by him all things consist.

And he is the head of the body, the church: who is the beginning, the firstborn from the dead; that in all things he might have the pre-eminence.

For it pleased the Father that in him should all fulness dwell;

Colossians 1:13-19

The Tapestry of the Kingdom

We conclude, thankfully, that indeed *"all fulness"* shall *"dwell"* in Him. The multi-colored threads spun before

Eden's arboretum have even now been woven into the tapestry of the kingdom story. From the black thread of buried treasure, to the bright blue of prophecy's promises, to the purples and browns of historic Israel, to the living vibrant gold of the *"Israel of God"*, intertwined with the blood red thread of redemption's life line, the tapestry hangs before us.

BOOK II

CHAPTER 11

The Search

There's an old joke in Israel. Moses wandered the desert for forty years and settled in the only spot in the Middle East that had no oil. This joke has become a stinging epithet of Israel's search for oil within its borders.

Beginnings

Limited exploration from 1900 until 1948 turned up little but the belief that oil may lie somewhere in the south; possibly beneath the Dead Sea or the Northern Negev desert. European powers attracted to the Middle East's oil producing potential spent the last part of the nineteenth and first part of the twentieth centuries tussling over and divvying up territories in the region based on their individual power and interests. The British controlled Palestine and a good bit of the rest of the Middle East during this period and exploration contracts were issued and controlled under their mandate. IPC (Iraqi Petroleum Company), a British controlled European consortium including BP (British Petroleum), Shell (Anglo/Dutch), Elf (French), Exxon and Mobil, showed interest in the Heletz area of southern Palestine; a part of the northern Negev desert.

IPC drilled the first oil exploration well in Israel (then Palestine), named Hulikhat, in 1947. Political violence related to Israel's upcoming independence was heating up in the area and IPC was forced to stop drilling before their target depth was reached. In the 1930's IPC was also responsible for the construction of an oil pipeline from the Kirkuk oilfields in northern Iraq to the port of Haifa in Palestine. At that time virtually all of the Middle East was under British or French influence so the idea of an oil pipeline from Iraq, through land that would later become Syria, Jordan and Israel to the Mediterranean Ocean seemed like a safe and economically reasonable method of transporting oil to waiting tankers at the port of Haifa. The creation of independent Arab and Jewish states after World War II, however, forever stalled future Arab oil flowing to Haifa. The idea of Arab oil flowing to world markets through Israel was not an alternative Arab producers considered open for discussion. In the short span of Israel's history the pipeline has remained empty.

Independence

On May 14, 1948 Israel became an independent state, and immediately cancelled all oil licenses granted under British Mandate. Israel was born fighting. Her Arab neighbor enemies, now independent states themselves, vowed to push her into the sea on the day she was born. The moment the British authority pulled out they acted to make good on their vow. Israel, however, was not pushed into the sea by her enemies. Every time they attacked, Israel rebuffed, taking more territory with each enemy *"advance"*. Once her prognosis for survival as a nation moved from critical to guarded Israel turned her attention to building the infrastructure necessary to develop as an independent state. One of the foundations of infrastructure is energy and one of the primary sources of energy is oil. In 1952 the Israeli Petroleum Law was enacted.

The Israeli Petroleum Law

The Israeli Petroleum Law states that *"petroleum resources belong to the State."* These State owned resources extend beyond the land itself to include Israel's territorial waters. The Law governs all exploration and production of all petroleum products. The Law provides three types of permits to explore for or produce petroleum in the country. The first *"preliminary permit"* allows the holder to conduct initial prospecting in the permit area with the exception of drilling. This eighteen month permit also gives the holder the privilege of requesting a *"priority right"* on the permit area. The priority right prevents the awarding the area's petroleum rights to anyone else during the term of the permit. The second permit stage is a three to four year *"exploration license"*. This license allows for drilling of test wells in an area of not more than 400,000 dunams (100,000 acres). If and when a prospector discovers oil in economically retrievable quantities under the exploration license he may apply for a *"production lease"*. The production lease term is thirty years, extendable to fifty years.

Just because a company has been granted a license to explore for or produce oil in an area doesn't give them access to the area. Once granted a permit, license, or lease, the holder must also secure permission from other State agencies and property owners to actually conduct activities in the license area. The holder is also required to submit regular progress reports and final reports to Ministry of Infrastructure. All research, test results, studies and any other information produced through exploration efforts are to be submitted to the Ministry as the property of the state. The production lease gives the lessee the right to market any petroleum produced, subject to the State of Israel preempting the petroleum for its own use. The State also collects a 12 ½% royalty on all petroleum produced. All in all, Israel's petroleum law is an effective method of allowing outside commercial entities (the licensees) to finance the exploration and production of oil in the country. Israel benefits by having access to all the exploration data and 12 ½% of all the oil produced.

Drilling

In 1955 the Hulikhat well, Israel's first ever, was reopened and Israel was in the oil business. Hulikhat produced a steady, but modest flow of oil and became the premier well in what came to be known as the *"Heletz Oil Field Discovery"*. The Heletz field has produced 18 million barrels of oil (virtually all of Israel's domestic production) since its opening in 1955. Heletz still in production today but the flow is now a trickle and its reserves are nearly exhausted. The country's other big energy find was the Zohar gas field, also in the northern Negev, just a stone's throw from Heletz. The Zohar gas field has produced 30 billion cubic feet of gas to date but she too is showing signs of old age. Heletz and Zohar production, never world class, are today marginal at best. As the new millennium was dawning a welcomed discovery brightened Israel's energy future. Gas, and plenty of it, was discovered off the coast of Ashkelon and Gaza. Gas isn't oil; but it isn't bad! Estimated reserves at 3.5 trillion cubic feet are a boon to Israel's energy future. Today Israel's offshore gas is slated to replace oil in all oil fueled electrical generating stations in the country.

Israel was lucky early on with the Heletz and Zohar discoveries. The recent offshore gas field discovery provides the fuel needed for much of the country's electrical power, but new petroleum discoveries have been somewhere between spread-out and non-existent. If Israel had oil under the surface, as a lot of folks believed she did, she sure was having difficulty finding it. The northern Negev had always been a focal point for Israeli oil and gas exploration because of the early wins with Heletz and Zohar. Maybe it was time to look elsewhere.

The Dead Sea

The Dead Sea was another area of early interest for oil exploration. As far back as written records date, historical mention of tar pits in the Dead Sea area is common. Genesis 14:10 states:

> *Now the Valley of Siddim was full of tar pits, and when the kings of Sodom and Gomorrah fled, some of the men fell into them and the rest fled to the hills.*

The Greek geographer, Strabo (63 BC–21 AD) noted that:

> *Near the area of Masada, liquid pitch could be observed dropping out of the rocks. Vapours arose from the Dead Sea, itself, that ignited very easily. Sodom and Gomorrah being destroyed by fire; fires are seen in the area. This country is full of fire.*

The Dead Sea had always been considered rich in minerals and with all of the historical references to open tar pits this seemed surely an ideal place to look for oil. Petroleum prospectors figured that where there's pitch, there's oil. Unfortunately, the supposed connection has yet to prove any marketable results. The Dead Sea was also believed by some evangelical Christian oil men to be God's favorite spot. One of the more flamboyant evangelicals, a ten gallon hat wearing Texas oil man on a mission to *"discover oil for God and Israel"* got a lot of press but came up short when it came to actually finding petroleum. Texan, Christian, Jew or just plain oil man, it seems that the Dead Sea gamble came up dry for everyone. In the last of a series of articles about a major Dead Sea oil exploration effort in the early 1990's, Israel Business Today gave a brief summary of the hunt for Dead Sea oil.

> *The oil exploration project at the Sdom Amok 1 drill site near the Dead Sea has been*

suspended following no signs of oil...The Sdom Amok project is the deepest and most expensive oil drill ever conducted in Israel. The companies involved have spent $20 million on the drilling and another $3 million on production tests. Drills have been conducted to a maximum depth of 6.4 km and could be extended as deep as 7.5 km. According to published reports, the drilling equipment which has been at Sdom Amok since the beginning of 1992 will be dismantled and reassembled at a site in the Besor region of the northwestern Negev...[2]

The Bible Prospectors

Israel's early focus on oil exploration had always been in the south. The Negev and Dead Sea kept the attention of Israel's oil prospectors, legitimate and illegitimate. The country's northern territories were outside of the spotlight of official attention, but the north country was the center of focus for a different group of *"oil hunters"*. This group was different in that the information that gave birth to their search came from a unique source. The information and maps used by oil hunters in the north came from the pages of the Bible. Specifically citing passages in Genesis and Deuteronomy, they understood phrases like *"...Out of Asher his bread shall be fat..." "...blessings of the deep that lieth under..."* and *"...let him dip his foot in oil..."* to mean that God had promised the children of Israel a vast treasure of oil and provided clues as to where it was located. The oil, according to these Bible based hunters, was beneath specific tribal territories of Jacob's children.

---

[2] Back to proven territory in the Northern Negev

Asher's Oil and Elijah's Water

Bible based oil explorers showed up in Israel as early as 1961. According to Moshe Goldberg, Israel's former Oil Commissioner, an American who was convinced that oil could be found in the land of the ancient tribe of Asher.[3] Armed with a report forecasting Israel's oil potential, and *"Asher"* passages, the *"Bible Prospector"* was granted an exploration license in Northern Israel. The license area included Mount Carmel and extended into parts of the Jezreel Valley, known as the *"Valley of Megiddo"*, site of the prophesied last day battle of Armageddon.

Another Bible story tied the Mount Carmel area to the promise of petroleum. Elijah, the prophet of Jehovah, was coerced into a contest with the local prophets of Baal. Baal's spokesmen, failing to convince their god to receive a sacrifice by consuming it with fire, allow Elijah to entreat his God to consume his sacrifice. Having taunted the prophets of Baal throughout the morning for their failed attempts, Elijah has a final one-upmanship planned. He fills four large jars with water and drenches his alter and sacrifice. Repeating this soaking twice more, Elijah then asks Jehovah to prove Himself. Fire immediately comes down from heaven and consumes not only the sacrifice and the wood but the alter and surrounding soil as well. In the minds of some early *"Bible Prospectors"* Elijah's *"water"* from Mount Carmel was really naturally occurring liquid petroleum, thus the conflagration. One early oil prospector reportedly went so far as to *"rebuild"* Elijah's alter on Mount Carmel in memory of the event. After a series of unproductive wells, the early Mount Carmel prospectors went home, never finding Asher's *"oil"* or Elijah's *"water"*.

---

[3] "With Rebbe's Blessing, Israel Drills for Oil", A.P. Jerusalem, September 10, 2004

Gilman Hill

In 1979 Gilman Hill, another American evangelical Christian, came to Israel looking for Asher's oil. Unlike other Christian oil hunters, Gilman didn't rely on Old Testament passages or tribal maps to locate a well site. According to Hill, God directed him to drill for oil and showed him the well's location during a 1978 tour of Mount Carmel. Sponsored by Utah's Mount Carmel Trust, Gil had completed preliminary geological surveys and fulfilled permit requirements to begin drilling by 1980.

The government of Israel has always kept an interest on where the money to fund foreign oil prospectors was coming from. In Gilman Hill's case, they were very interested in just who was behind the Mount Carmel Trust. Interviewing Gillman on the subject, then Israeli Energy Minister Moday wanted to know specifically, just who was behind the Trust. *"Is there Israeli money involved in this project?"* Moday asked.

"No", was Hills response.

"Is there American Jewish money involved in this project?" inquired Moday. Again, Hill's reply was negative. Growing impatient, Moday asked finally, *"Are American Christians funding this project?"*

Gilman's response again was, *"No"*. Frustrating Moday further, Gilman offered a cryptic explanation, *"The Trust has two partners. I am a 1% partner, my associate is a 99% partner I have no financial ownership in the Trust, it is funded completely by my partner. I do, however, speak and act on his behalf and I have complete power of attorney for the Trust."*

Impressed but no more informed than before, Moday continued, *"Can you arrange for me to meet your partner?"*

"I would be delighted to introduce you to him," Gilman replied. *"My partner is the God of Abraham, Isaac,*

and Jacob; I am sure he would be very interested in you meeting him."

Realizing that he had been bested and would get no further on the subject, he completed the interview, *"Mr. Hill, you are a Christian and I am a Jew; but everyday I will pray for your success with this project."*

Shaking hands with Moday as he was leaving Hill offered Moday a final reply, *"Mr. Moday, you are a Jew and I am a Christian; but every day I will pray for you and for your success in the position God has placed you."* From that point forward Hill's relationship with the State of Israel and with Energy Minister Moday was secure.

Gilman Hill's well, Elijah I, was to be drilled to the upper Triassic strata, a depth of 15,000 to 16,000 feet. At 8,900 feet Gilman halted the drilling. According to Hill, God had told him to stop. Receiving the Divine message, *"circumstances have changed,"* Gil was convinced that he was to cease drilling until further notice from God. Frustrated that he was first led by God to begin drilling in Israel, then led to stop drilling without explanation. Gil continued his geologic research for another six years waiting for the Divine release to resume drilling. The release never came.

Gil continued working in Israel while he waited; adding to his geologic research. During his time in Israel Gil also began a successful prison ministry and proposed a water resource program that would supply southern Lebanon and northern Israel with sufficient water to ensure long term agricultural prosperity. The Elijah 1 well, however, was never to be reopened. After spending $6 million of his own money on Mount Carmel, drawn by the Bible's promise that Asher would *"dip his foot in oil",* he had failed to find the elusive flow. To his credit, and unfortunately not in keeping with some other American Christian *"oil men",* Gil quietly paid all of the debts associated with his project and went home. Today, in Israel, when the subject of American

Christians and oil comes up, Gilman Hill is remembered honorably.

Andy SoRelle

About the same time Hill started drilling Elijah 1, a Texas oil man named Andy SoRelle was busy preparing the Atlit 1 well near Haifa, known as the Asher Project. SoRelle first visited Israel in 1968 as part of a thirteen nation tour. As is common with Christian pilgrims to the Holy Land, Andy developed a connection with the land and people of Israel. Being an evangelical Christian, he was interested in the spiritual and political future of Israel. As an oil man, his visit also birthed a concern in his heart for the problem of Israel's oil future. He wondered at the seeming lack of oil exploration efforts in the country. The Heletz field in the Negev was active, but it consisted of shallow sand wells. He couldn't believe Heletz was a substantial long term answer to Israel's oil supply. Andy returned home from his 1968 tour with the seed of Israel and its oil future planted in his soul.

His next opportunity to do something about Israel's oil future came in 1976. Energy Exploration, Inc. SoRelle's Houston based company, had just developed a new technology for detecting petroleum deposits. *"Radio Metrics"* measured isotopic emissions radiating from potential petroleum deposits. SoRelle wrote to the Israeli government, offering to prospect in Israel, at his own expense, using his new technology. After month's had passed and frustrated by the skepticism and lack of response from Israel, SoRelle drafted a harshly worded letter to the Israeli government regarding their failure to accept an offer for free services to their benefit. Apparently the strong sentiments got their attention. Israel sent an oil expert to Houston to determine SoRelle's validity and check out his new technology.

Two weeks after the Israeli's visit SoRelle was invited to prospect for oil in Israel. In the autumn of 1977 Andy returned to Israel with his Radio Metric equipment. After poor showings at several INOC (Israel National Oil Company) sites, Andy moved his equipment, at the government's request, to the Sinai. Within a few weeks, using his Radio Metric equipment, he found a site with high probability of oil. Andy immediately applied for an exploration permit in the Sinai. Unfortunately, at the same time Anwar Sadat of Egypt was traveling to Jerusalem in hope of regaining the Sinai from Israel, who had taken the land from Egypt during the 1973 Yom Kippur War. Peace talks put further oil exploration in the area on hold. Andy was stuck on hold for two years while Egypt and Israel worked through a peace plan. In March of 1979 the Israel-Egypt Peace Treaty was signed as the first realization of the 1978 Camp David Peace Accords. Provisions in the treaty called for Israel to return possession of the Sinai to Egypt. Andy SoRelle's plans for drilling in the Sinai went from *"on-hold"* to non-existent.

Undaunted, Andy discovered another approach to finding oil in Israel. Using Deuteronomy 32:24 and a Bible map of Israel's ancient tribal lands as his guides he returned to Israel to find the oil the Bible had promised in the *"foot of Asher."* Speaking with Israel's chief geologist, he learned that the ancient tribal land of the foot of Asher, the area between Haifa and Caesarea, was the only part of Israel that hadn't been surveyed by oil explorers. Andy applied for, and was granted a 100,000 acre exploration license *"block 174 Carmel Coast"*, named *"The Asher Project"* by SoRelle.

Andy SoRelle's first and only well, the Atlit1, was spudded (drilling begun) in February 1981, the same year Jim Spillman's original book about Israel's oil, ***The Great Treasure Hunt***, was released. Spillman and SoRelle were mutual supporters, each understandably interested in the work of the other. Throughout SoRelle's career in Israel he updated Spillman on the progress of the well they both believed would strike the oil God had promised to Jacob's children nearly 4,000 years earlier.

The Atlit 1 well, located just inside Israel's Atlit Naval Base and adjacent to the ruins of a crusader castle was plagued with drilling problems from its beginning. Clearing the drill rig site, a bulldozer uncovered rooftops from an ancient crusader city believed to have been built the same time as the castle. Additionally, archaeologists discovered that the crusader city had been built on top of an earlier Phoenician city. Atlit 1 became an historical treasure overnight. In order to preserve any ancient artifacts that may lie directly below the drilling area SoRelle and Israel's Antiquities Ministry came to a compromise. Rather than grade the site for the drill rig, Andy agreed to fill the drill site, therefore preserving any artifacts that may lay beneath the existing grade of the land. This compromise cost SoRelle an additional $60,000.

The drill rig, an Ideco Super 711, was rated to a depth of 15,000 feet. At 9,400 feet the dill bit hit volcanic rock. Volcanic flows of 700 to 1,000 feet thick were a common occurrence so hitting this stratum didn't surprise anyone. Their surprise came as they drilled continually deeper, without breaking out of the volcanic layer. They drilled down through another 7600 feet of volcanic rock before finally coming into limestone again. The Ideco drill rig now at 17,296 feet was way beyond its capacity. Fearing he would lose the hole and the rig, Atlit's drilling supervisor, Vic Lambert, shut down the operation until a larger rig could be brought in.

December 28, 1982, more than a year after the drilling at Atlit I had been suspended, the new Lapidoth Emsco 1500 drill rig, rated at 26,000 feet was installed over the original hole. This new phase, named Atlit II was planned to bring the well to a depth of as much as 23,000 feet. By February of 1983 the well had been cleaned out and depth had been increased to 18,000 feet. Drilling continued without incident until, at 20,570 feet Atlit II struck oil! What oil experts call *"very good shows"* came to the surface; graded as light oil at 35 to 40 degrees API; very good stuff! SoRelle continued to a final depth of 21,431 feet. The *"pay zone"*, the depth of hole actually producing oil was estimated at 470 feet, from 20,570 to 21,309 feet of total depth. The drilling of Atlit II was finally complete! Now it was time to develop the well (prepare the hole and the site for production).

During the development phase problems emerged again. Financing for the project had been shoe-string at best for quite some time. The crew had stopped casing the well at 13,772 feet. Casing is the steel sleeve installed as the hole is drilled, to keep it from caving in on itself. On the Atlit I phase 13 3/8 inch casing was installed to 2,742 feet, then a smaller 9 5/8 inch casing to 4,643 feet, finally a 7 inch casing to 13,732 feet. After 13,732 feet the casing stopped. Not having funds for additional casing and reasoning that the volcanic flow they had struggled through was stable enough to hold the hole open the crew continued drilling in *"open hole"*, without casing. *Drilling Magazine*, in its October 1984 issue describes the heartbreaking events that happened during the development phase.

> *The decision was made to go for a completion which included setting a 5-in. liner in the open hole section and perforating the pay zone. Special 5-in. pipe was shipped to Haifa, and the crew was cleaning the hole in preparation when more trouble struck. Tripping out, the drill collars stuck at 18,669 ft and two weeks of jarring would not break them loose. Special equipment was flown in from the U.S. to retrieve the fish (130 ft. in length) and, while cleaning the hole to "fish" with the new equipment they stuck again at the 17,772 ft mark. After ten more days of*

trying to break loose, they came out leaving another 8 ½ ft fish in the hole.

August 24, 1983, more than two and a half years after spudding, Andy SoRelle called it quits for the Atlit hole. At $20,000 a day in drilling expenses, the money had run out, and after two catastrophic bad luck events the hole was permanently closed. Having spent more than $25 million on the project, his own money and that of his investors, Andy gave up on the hole; but he never surrendered his dream of discovering Asher's oil.

Andy SoRelle was out of money and, at sixty-four years old, he felt the project had also taken its toll on him personally. Atlit I and Atlit II had spent more than his money. The last three years had exhausted his physical resources as well. His indomitable spirit, however, was still intact. SoRelle did what most wildcat oil men do when faced with irrecoverable losses and shattering disappointment, he began planning for a new drill site - Atlit III. Andy returned to the States to raise money for Atlit III but the funding proved elusive. His investors, oil men, business professionals and church groups, had trusted him with money for Atlit I and Atlit II. Why should they think he wouldn't come up dry on Atlit III as well? *"God may have promised oil to Israel's children,"* they reasoned, *"but was Andy the man God had chosen to deliver it?"*

Lack of money, poor health, and growing Palestinian violence have all been cited as reasons for the still birth of Atlit III. Whatever the reasons, the time and individual had not yet arrived for the discovery of oil in Israel.

Tovia Luskin

Want to hear a funny story? It involves a Jew and a Rabbi, but leaves out the Priest entirely. The story begins with a series of questions.

✡ What if G_d[4] set aside a vast oil treasure for the Children of Israel to be discovered in the lasts days?

✡ What if He left clues in the words of the Torah and in the land of Israel itself?

✡ What if these clues were published in a book by a popular American evangelical Christian minister and taken to heart by a diverse bunch of American evangelical Christian oil men?

✡ What if each of them traveled to Israel as G_d's man to give Israel its vast oil inheritance?

✡ What if they all failed, spending a lot of their own and other people's money in the quest?

✡ What if a Russian Jew, with the blessing of a New York Rabbi goes to Israel and actually discovers the oil G_d promised to Israel's Children?

Meet Tovia Luskin. Like his evangelical Christian American counterparts Tovia has been searching for oil in Israel for a long time now - seventeen years. Like his evangelical Christian American counterparts, Tovia uses the Bible (the Torah) as his guide and impetus for finding oil in the Holy Land. Unlike his evangelical Christian American counterparts, he isn't an evangelical Christian or an American. Also, unlike his evangelical American Christian counterparts, he has actually discovered the oil promised to the Children of Israel in Genesis and Deuteronomy!

Luskin, a Russian Jew and geologist, earned degrees in geophysics at Moscow State University. As a former lead geologist for Shell Oil and advisor to Bridge Oil in Sydney,

---

[4] Jewish law does not permit the speaking or writing of G_d's name except in prayer. Respecting this tradition, the current section uses the omitted vowel spelling.

Australia, his extensive background in the oil industry gave him the professional credence to back up his religious conviction that there was indeed, oil in Israel.

Working in Australia in 1988, Tovia, new as a practicing Jew, came upon a passage in the Torah in Deuteronomy. Tovia is naturally quiet about sharing his religious beliefs concerning the oil with skeptics who would use them to discount his professional and technical efforts in the project. But to those sincerely interested, he happily quotes from memory the passage that began his quest,

> *About Joseph, he (Moses) said: "May the Lord bless his land with the precious dew from heaven above and the deep waters that lie below; with the best the sun brings forth and the finest the moon can yield; with the choicest gifts of the ancient mountains and the fruitfulness of the everlasting hills..."*
>
> (Deut. 33:13 NIV)

This passage in Deuteronomy along with his discovery that the medieval Jewish scholar Rashi interpreted the passage to mean that the *"everlasting hills"* were much older than the surrounding countryside was proof that he was on to something. Rashi's interpretation struck home with Luskin. He knew, as a geologist, that the concept of one geological feature (the hills) being of a different age than the geography surrounding it was an accepted fundamental of modern geological science. But this concept was unknown in the time Rashi wrote his interpretation. In Luskin's view, Rashi had no way of interpreting the passage this way other than by divine guidance.

These two proofs were enough for him to write to Rebbe Menachem Mendel Schneerson, one of the world's renowned Jewish scholars, for his review and consideration of the interpretations. After reviewing his material, the

Rebbe, responded noting, *"I had pleasure in reading your discussion ..."* and *"... You will tell me good news ..."* This was enough for Luskin to get serious about taking action. He traveled to New York for a personal audience with the Rebbe. The Rebbe pronounced over him a bracha (blessing) regarding his proposed search for oil in the Promised Land, *"You have my blessing that you will have good news in the near future."* This innocuous sounding blessing carried tremendous authority for Luskin, believing the Rebbe to be G_d's Moshiach (Messiah), the one to bring redemption to the Jews. This was enough for Luskin to sell his home in Sydney, Australia and immigrate to Israel.

By 1993 Tovia Luskin had united an impressive team of geologists and oil experts (most of them Russian from his previous acquaintance at Moscow Sate University) to form Givot Olam Oil Exploration, LLC. Givot Olam, Hebrew for *"everlasting hills"*, secured a 62,500 acre exploration license just north and east of Tel Aviv. Their first well, the Meged 2, was drilled in 1994 and successfully tested 40° API oil at 17,000 feet. In 1998 the Meged 2 was retested and showed a 400 barrel per day flow rate. The Meged 3 well was drilled two years later a few miles to the west of the Meged 2. This well logged 47 feet of pay (the vertical area of the well from which to extract oil) at 15,000 feet deep, but had to be shut down because of mechanical problems in the hole. The Meged 4, north of the Meged 2 and Meged 3, was drilled in 2003. At 16,000 feet the Meged 4 began flowing oil and gas. The rate of flow was unspecified but Givot Olam reported a commercial discovery of 980 million barrels. With the Meged 4 discovery the Givot Olam eighteen month exploration license became a thirty year production lease.

Today Givot Olam is in the process of developing the Meged Oil Field with plans for 10 wells in a 50 square kilometer project area. With proper development each well is conservatively estimated to produce over 900 barrels per day for the first year, and then decline to a steady 400 barrels per day over each well's seven year expected lifespan. The ten wells in this field, roughly one-fifth of Givot Olam's production lease area, in the conservative view is capable of producing over 12 million barrels of oil over the next seven years. Israel has only produced 20 million barrels in its entire fifty year history of oil production! Personally Luskin estimates the Givot Olam lease area to hold as many as a billion barrels of oil. Twenty percent of those billion barrels, Luskin believes, is recoverable. Two hundred million barrels at $50.00 or more a barrel adds up to ten billion dollars. Not bad for Jewish Russian immigrant using the Torah and his Rebbe's blessing as a guide!

Chapter 12

John Brown and Zion Oil

John Brown is a man of faith; he takes God at his word…literally. He wasn't always this way, however. In 1981 John's life was that of a fast track executive for a rapidly growing Michigan cutting tool company. Non-stop work, private jets, free flowing money, and free flowing booze brought John to a crisis point in his life. The pace, the work, the money and the booze in his life had taken a toll on the people around him. Troubled over his rip-tear lifestyle and increasing alcoholism, John's wife and business partners pushed him to get help. Help for John, however, came from a direction no one around him expected. His alcoholism may have brought him to a place of crisis; but for his family and colleagues the real disaster came when John found the cure.

John Brown met God. John's personal conversion led to an instant and complete polar change. One day he was rip-tear, heavy drinking John Brown. His partners were worried, his wife was fed up; he was a pain, but at least he was a pain they recognized. When John met God, accepted His Son as savior, and committed his life to whatever God had for him, he became a man his wife and colleagues definitely didn't recognize. The new John had no taste for booze or the wild life; in their eyes, this was a good thing. But…there was something else they weren't so comfortable with. John had become a believer - a born again, dyed in the wool, utterly shameless, really fanatical, true believer. John witnessed to everyone, everywhere! He told them how God had saved him, delivered him from alcoholism, brought hope and joy and purpose into his life. At work he told everyone in his path about Jesus and his love. Handing out cards that said, *"JESUS LOVES YOU"* on the front, with instructions for *"How to Make Heaven Your Home"* on the back, John asked people if they were saved; and if the answer was no, he'd ask, did they want to be! His colleagues didn't know what to do with him. In the business, he was becoming the guy to be avoided.

If the reaction at work was bad, the one at home was worse. John's wife definitely saw a change; and she just couldn't reconcile herself with the new man. Yesterday she was sure that her husband would drink or work himself to death. Today she had a religious fanatic to deal with. She couldn't cope with this new man and his message of Jesus, and love, and salvation. The man was scarier now than when he was drinking! She knew there was only one solution to a problem this big. It was time to get the church involved.

The problem with new converts, especially *"true believers"* like John is that they lack the restraint with which the church has so well equipped those fortunate enough to have been raised from birth in her loving bosom. When he met with their priest John actually had the gall to ask him if he knew Jesus! If he knew Jesus?! If he knew Jesus?! He was a priest! He was the man God (or at least the pope) assigned as a shepherd to this flock; one of whom was now inquiring if he knew Jesus! The man was obviously a fanatic, unschooled in the church; barely attended mass; and now he wants to know if his appointed shepherd knows Jesus? This was a problem. This new convert (probably protestant) was obviously overcome by religious zeal, unwilling to listen to reason, and unwilling to accept the priest's authority as his appointed spiritual leader. This was dangerous. This man, pursuing his current course of unrestrained evangelism could damage the circumspect reputation of the parish and subsequently destroy his family's standing in the church. The decision was harsh, but for the betterment of the church, the eternal security of his family and the safety of the kingdom drastic action had to be taken. With the blessing of John's wife, the priest arranged for a religious annulment. In the eyes of the church John Brown no longer had a wife or children. In the eyes of the church, the new convert, the man who had met Jesus face to face, no longer existed. John Brown was excommunicated. In the stroke of a pen he lost his family and his church; for the safety of the kingdom.

The Vision

John Brown, however, was a true believer. He knew what he knew. Meeting God was real; the most real thing that had ever happened to him. Nothing was going to change that. Soon after his run-in with the Catholic Church John Brown experienced another life changing event. Jim Spillman was invited to speak at his new church in Clawson, Michigan. Spillman told his audience that he had felt compelled to accept this invitation, canceling vacation plans in order to share a very unique message with this group at this time. Jim Spillman told of a promise God made to Jacob's (Israel's) children almost four thousand years ago, to bless them in the last days. Hidden in the words of Jacob's blessing and revealed in the boundaries delineating Israel's ancient lands lay the clues to finding an incredible treasure. A treasure map, taught Spillman, was drafted into the words of the Bible and set into the tribal boundaries of a people who had not yet entered into their promised land. The treasure, a vast oil reserve, was waiting to be discovered in the *"latter years"* to fulfill God's purpose and provide for his people, Israel. John listened patiently. At first the idea seemed doubtful. But, Jim's logic, knowledge of the original language of the Bible and stack of supporting evidence made a convincing argument that God had deposited oil in Israel for some last days purpose. Hooked, John left the church in Clawson that night with the seed of a vision planted in his heart.

John Brown was a true believer (*have I mentioned that?*). He knew now, without doubt that the Bible promised a vast treasure of oil for Israel in the last days and pointed to its location. There was oil in Israel and John knew where to find it. This knowledge and his unquestioning faith nurtured the vision seed that would incubate in John's soul for the next two years.

I asked John recently what Jim Spillman and that night in Clawson meant to him. Following John's train of thought was an adventure, as he bounced along a rapid fire idea trail jumping in and out of scripture passages to get the fullness of his meaning across. Starting and ending with Bible quotes, John referred to Jim's passing and remembered the effect his message had on his life over the last twenty-four years.

> *"Then I heard a voice from heaven say, 'Write: Blessed are the dead who die in the Lord from now on.' 'Yes,' says the Spirit, 'they will rest from their labor, for their deeds follow with them.'" (Revelation 14:13)*

> *One of Jim's deeds will be that the revelation that God gave him about the oil of Israel in the '70's will shortly come to pass. Why? Because God sent Jim to Zion temple in Clawson, Michigan in February 1981. Jim taught us the scriptures that proved that oil would someday be found in Israel and on the head of Joseph! It was during Jim's teaching that God first deposited the vision in my heart about the oil in Israel and by faith; I believed it (Hebrews 11:1). "Consequently, faith comes from hearing the message, and the message is heard through the words of Christ" (Romans. 10:17). Jim Spillman obeyed God and delivered the message to me in 1981. That vision and God's promises are now coming to pass in Israel. "For the revelation awaits an appointed time; it speaks*

of the end and will not prove false. Though it linger, wait for it; it will certainly come and not delay." (Habakkuk 2:3)

Praying for Oil

According to John, God specifically told him to go to Israel in May of 1983. John's friend and mentor, Alger Wolfe accompanied him with the intention of introducing him to an old friend from Texas, Andy SoRelle. SoRelle was an oilman and had been drilling in Israel, near Haifa for the last two years. Like Brown, SoRelle had also heard Jim Spillman's *"Treasure"* message and set the location of his well site to be in the area known as the *"foot of Asher"*.

During this first trip to Israel John felt God directing him to a specific portion of scripture. Finding his Bible, he paged through the Old Testament until he found the passage. It was in the book of I Kings, describing the dedication of the first temple in Jerusalem. The passage came from Solomon's prayer of dedication:

> *Moreover concerning a stranger, that is not of thy people Israel, but cometh out of a far country for thy name's sake: (for they shall hear of thy great name, and of thy strong hand, and of thy stretched out arm); when he shall come and pray towards this house; hear thou in heaven thy dwelling place, and do according to all that the stranger calleth to thee for: that all the people of the earth might know thy name, to fear thee, as do thy people Israel and that they might know that this house, which I have builded, is called by thy name.*
>
> (8:41-43)

John believed that he was the stranger and the far country he came from was America, his home. He believed that if he prayed toward God's temple in Jerusalem, like the passage read, God would hear and do according to what he, the stranger, prayed so that the world would know that God honors His temple. John asked God for the oil he had deposited there millions of years earlier, and promised to Israel nearly four thousand years ago. John wanted the oil, not for himself, but for the people and land of Israel. Armed with the scripture God had given him and the faith that it would happen. John knew that he would be the one to discover the Israel's oil.

The facts facing him were irrelevant; John stood on the promise he was given. The facts that John was a Michigan tool maker and knew nothing about oil exploration and little about the state of Israel didn't seem to be an obstacle for him. The facts that he had no contacts in the oil business or in Israel didn't bother him a bit. Citing another Bible passage, Mark 11:22–24, he states, *"...by faith I believed I received it ...and since then I have by faith spoken it and <u>do not</u> doubt it"*.

Letter of Resignation

Returning to Michigan from his visit to Israel, there was something John had to do. John drafted, in faith, an open letter of resignation to the people of the company he helped found. Just when they thought they were getting accustomed to the *"new"* John, his business associates were thrown for another loop by their resident *"Believer"*. The letter left very little doubt about where he stood personally and spiritually, and what he intended to do with the remainder of his life.

June 1983

TO ALL MY FRIENDS AT GTE VALERON

    Now it is with deep regret that I must resign from GTE Valeron. However, I am involved in an oil project that God blessed me with in Israel, and now will devote all of my time in the oil business and doing God's work. Most of you are familiar or know of my past when I was hospitalized four (4) times for alcoholism, but this was all changed dramatically in January 1981 when I was "Saved" or "Born Again". These two (2) terms are not from any denomination, but it is from the Bible and can be found in the New Testament in the book of St. John, Chapter 3 verses 3 through 7. What these terms mean is that I accepted JESUS CHRIST as my <u>Personal Savior</u>. I can testify that I have sat in churches all my life, but I was not "Saved" or "Born Again".

    There is no church membership or denomination or water baptism whereby you are "Born Again" or "Saved", and there is Salvation <u>in no other way</u> but for each person to individually accept JESUS CHRIST as their own personal Savior and Lord of their life. Like St. Paul in the New Testament, I was instantly converted and I believe it was to be a witness for you especially here at GTE Valeron. Please don't misunderstand me, as I am not anything special nor did I earn the Salvation, because it cannot be earned as it is a universal gift of God and available to everyone who wants it.

    I now pray that each and every one of you will believe that what happened to me is <u>very real</u> and seek the truth for yourselves. Please don't ignore what God is saying to you through me because it is a <u>clear choice</u> whether you choose JESUS CHRIST as your Personal Savior and receive eternal Salvation, or deny Him and Choose eternal damnation.

I love you all and that is why I'm sending you this.

IN HIS LOVE,

John Brown

John Brown

Testimony JB

    John may have worked the longest notice in history. Two years after he submitted his resignation John left his position at Valeron to devote his full attention to his dream. His vision of discovering oil in Israel became a full-time quest in December of 1985.

Houston

During his time in Michigan John met and married Joan Gray. In typical God to John Brown style, he knew at first glance that she was to be his wife. Fortunately, God gave Joan and their pastors similar information. By the time they moved to Houston, Texas in 1986 Joan had adopted John's vision in her own way and was ready to go when they were called. From the day they were married through today Joan prays every day for the state of Israel and its people.

The move to Houston, according to John, was again, under specific orders from God. He likens the experience to Abraham being called by God away from his homeland to a place *"God would show him."* John still admits that he doesn't know all the reasons for going to Houston but a procession of providential events served to confirm that it was the right move.

Houston seemed like a reasonable place to be if you were in the oil business…even if the oil business you were to be in was in Israel. On that subject; it turned out that 1986 was not the best time to be in the oil business in Israel. At the beginning of the year the Israeli government elected to suspend all drilling operations in the country for two years in order to conduct a basin analysis study. Anyone in the oil drilling business in Israel was out of business until further notice.

A basin analysis study, simply put, describes the land in terms of geologic basins (where oil could possibly be) and details the history of exploration in the area (what people have done so far to find the oil). Fortunately for John, shutting down the oil exploration business in Israel for the first two years he was in the oil exploration business was the best thing that could have happened to him. Making several trips to Israel during the period, John met with government officials and hired industry consultants in Israel and Texas to conduct research in the area he knew the oil would be located; the land the Bible pointed to as *"the crown of the head of Joseph.*" During the study's *"down-time"* John received a first rate education in the oil business and created a series of crucial relationships that would establish him in Israel's oil exploration industry.

In 1990 John met Elisha Roih. If Israel could have sent a guardian angel to John Brown, he would have come in the form of Elisha Roih. Elisha's history was the history of Israel. Born a Palestinian Jew (a Jew born in Palestine before Israel existed as a State) Elisha was part of a small group of Jewish patriots, *"pre-Israelis"*, instrumental in the country's defense before, during and after her independence in 1948. Today *"retired"* Colonel Elisha Roih is still an active member of the Israeli Defense Forces. After forty years of experience as a manager in every government owned oil company in Israel Elisha showed up at John's door in Houston after receiving a letter asking for help. Amazed that one of Israel's oil pioneers would materialize on his doorstep in Houston, John asked incredulously, *"What are you doing here?"*

"I've come to help", Elisha replied. And that was it. Elisha *"adopted"* John and his mission to find oil in Israel; With Elisha's help, John was introduced and accepted into Israel's oil industry. Today, Elisha Roih serves as Vice President, Administration of Israeli Operations for Zion Oil & Gas, Inc.

Spending his own resources was a non-issue for John. From the time he first received the vision of finding oil in Israel through his last days in Houston John invested every dollar and every moment of his time in the search. Other people's resources were another matter entirely. John wasn't alone in underwriting his vision for finding oil in Israel but the group of friends willing to contribute money, time and prayers was small. A special friend, Ralph DeVore, helped and encouraged John from the beginning. In addition to being integral in raising seed capital for the new-born business, Ralph introduced John to his cousin, renowned prophecy teacher Hal Lindsay, who remains an avid and public supporter of the Zion Oil vision.

Raising money baffled John. Not the process of raising money, he understood that. He had raised money for business ventures in the past. What baffled John was the response he received from his audience. For him the issue was black and white. God put oil in Israel to bless its people, he showed us where the oil is; now we are to go and retrieve it. Surely anyone interested in Israel and her people could understand this logic and would enthusiastically underwrite the venture!

John went first to the Jewish community in the United States. His vision included seeing the people of Israel prosper as a result of this wonderful discovery. Surely the Jewish community in America would be the first to forward the prosperity of their brothers and sisters in Israel. Apparently that wasn't the case. Jews in America, for the most part, are in favor of a strong and prosperous Israel. They are the first and most prolific donors to the country's cause. Investing in an oil company founded by this gentile Zionist for the betterment of Israel, however, was not what they considered *"mitzvah"*. Mitzvah, is in Jewish terms, *"the law"*, the rules. If a Jew in America wants to help Israel, he gives directly to Israel; not to some Gentile Christian Zionist whose goal is to discover oil in Israel. That's mitzvah!

If America's Jews wouldn't understand and participate, what about America's Christians; surely they wanted to see Israel blessed by God through this great discovery? John went to the evangelical Christian community (Christians who believe that their mission is to spread the gospel of Christ). The response was mixed. Many Christians understood, believed and backed the effort. Others figured it was just another scam. Unfortunately, John wasn't the only one trying to convince American Christians to invest money in finding Israel's oil. There were others, some sincere, some flat out crooks, preaching the same gospel of investing in the search for Israel's oil. Investors lost their money; either through the principal's honest attempts and failure to discover oil; or through downright mismanagement and fraud. The fact was that investing in the search for oil in Israel from 1983 to 1996 was a bad deal. Everybody lost money. Investing money in a prophetic treasure hunt for oil in Israel also siphoned money and attention away from other *"more relevant"* missions for evangelical Christians in America, which in the opinion of John's critics, were whatever they deemed *"more relevant"* missions were for America's evangelical Christians at the moment. The hunt for oil in Israel became just another cause on a long list of Christian causes.

Ten years of full time vision quest for John Brown resulted in being broke, really broke, in Houston Texas. In the last ten years he had traveled to Israel six times. He had spent every dime he owned, which, at the beginning was a considerable amount of dimes, working to make the vision a reality. He had traveled the U.S. to tell his story and spread the vision. Now, in 1996, ten years after committing himself full-time to *"God's work"* he was broke, destitute, and stuck in Houston. John was done with the oil business, done with Israel, done with throwing all of his money, time and energy into a vision that always seemed just beyond his reach. He wanted to admit defeat, go home to Michigan, and pick up what was left of his life. Unfortunately, he was too broke to even give up and go home. The next several months of *"captivity"* in Houston gave John opportunity to reflect on the *"Vision"* and his whirlwind ride of promise, spending, and activity over the last ten years. It also gave John the opportunity to experience life at the end of his own strength and capital. He didn't have money for groceries; he certainly couldn't afford to pursue the promise of finding oil in Israel. If the oil was to be discovered and Israel was to be blessed, it was going to have to be someone else doing the discovering and blessing. John was done.

Back in Michigan, John's son, Mark was involved in a small concrete forming business. John didn't know anything about concrete forming and he didn't have the money to get back to Michigan. But, true to his history of living beyond the facts; enough cash for a one-way trip to Michigan miraculously materialized and John jumped into the concrete business. Within eighteen months the M&B companies had produced over $8 million in new sales, nearly $1 million in profits, and a $1.5 million credit line. During his time in Michigan, God made it clear to John that He had no intention of reneging on His promise and He refused to allow John to *"retire"* into the concrete business. John Brown, concrete man, was once again capitalized. It was time to renew his search for oil in Israel.

Zion Oil

John met Israeli attorney Philip Mandelker in 1998. Philip's background in petroleum law, both in the U.S. and Israel is extensive. He is regarded by his peers as one of Israel's premier oil and gas experts. Mandelker was instrumental in John's survival and growth in Israel's oil industry. With Philip's help, John formed Zion Oil & Gas, Inc. in April of 2000 and was awarded a small (28,800 acre) onshore petroleum license from the Israeli government.

Always eager to share with those around him, John included twenty-five friends and partners in the ownership of Zion. The initial cash contribution of $2400 became 2,400,000 shares of stock valued at 1/10 of one cent per share. John and his partners contributed all of the technical, economic, legal and financial information they had accumulated during the past fourteen years as owners' equity in the new company. They didn't put a dollar value on their experience and information but the real costs in direct investment and human effort would have been in the millions of dollars.

Their renewed vision of finding oil in Israel came into laser focus with the founding of Zion Oil & Gas, Inc. As the core of the company's Vision Statement (see Appendix B) Zion's Purpose Statement is direct and specific:

> *Zion Oil & Gas was ordained by G_d for the express purpose of discovering oil and gas in the land of Israel and to bless the Jewish people and the nation of Israel and the body of Christ.(Isaiah 23:18) I believe that G_d has promised in the Bible to bless Israel with one of the world's largest oil and gas fields and this will be discovered in the last days before the Messiah returns and that it will be found on the Ma'anit License and the Joseph permit, both being on the head of Joseph.*

In January of 2003 Zion was granted an extended license area, called the Ma'anit – Joseph License, totaling 95,800 acres. The map on the following page depicts an overlay of location of the Ma'anit – Joseph License area (shaded in gray) in relation to the ancient tribal territories of Israel. The license area lies just south of the *"foot of Asher"* and consists of a substantial portion of Manasseh's tribal boundaries, the *"crown of the head of Joseph"*. John Brown's vision had just burst forth into reality.

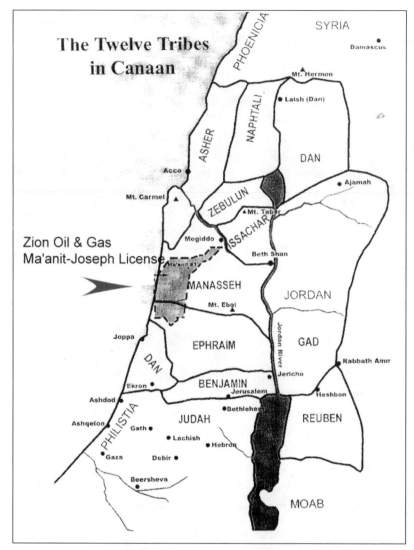

Assembling the Team

The founding of Zion Oil & Gas, Inc. attracted a group of professionals that, in any industry, could only be considered miraculous. The caliber and experience of the people drawn to Zion is a remarkable story in itself. Inexplicably drawn to the project, the oil industry's best, in

Israel and abroad somehow assembled to create an amazingly unique organization.

▶ **Gene Soltero** was introduced to John Brown and Zion Oil by Philip Mandelker in 1999. Today Gene serves as president and CEO of Zion Oil & Gas. Anyone else with his track record would seriously consider retiring. Gene has already enjoyed a fulfilling and lucrative career running a series of successful oil companies for more than thirty years. He can't say he hasn't contributed and he can't say he's not financially able to retire. He's more than covered those two points. Another good reason for Gene to retire is that he loves to sail. More accurately, Gene loves racing snipes. A snipe (not the legendary bird) is a small two-person sailboat. Factually, it's smaller than that. According to SCIRA, the Snipe Class International Racing Association, it's just a dinghy. And a dinghy, even landlubbers know, is a really, really small boat. A member of the Corinthian Sailing Club, Gene sails and races regularly at White Rock Lake, adjacent to his Dallas home in a comfortably well-to-do neighborhood bordering the lake. Not satisfied to limit his snipe experience to White Rock Lake, Gene often travels around the world to compete successfully in snipe regattas. Although it's rumored that snipe regattas are as popular for their related celebrations as for the racing, Gene is considered by his peers as a serious sailor. If the truth was known, there's a part of Gene that wishes he could spend more time sniping and less time running an oil exploration company.

So why would a serious snipe racer and oughta-be comfortably retired businessman postpone a fulfilling retirement for a risky pipe-dream like looking for oil in Israel? That was the question on my mind during an interview with Gene last year. After spending the day with Brown at Zion's Dallas office we drove to meet Gene at his home by the lake. Earlier that day I reviewed Gene's professional credentials and learned a little about his history. In this business, Gene had made his mark several times over. By oil industry standards this guy was world class. He had a long and consistent history of success in a very risky profession. What was attractive enough about Zion Oil to commit the next several years at this point in his life? I was about to find out.

Introduced to Gene for the first time I met a friendly and hospitable man, lacking any form of pretense that others of his professional stature may adopt. Still, he possessed the quiet, confident energy of a man very sure of who he was. His bald pate sported a rich tan betraying his time on the water and his smile radiated to the degree that I actually felt its warmth. When we had settled in his living room I was impatient to clear up my mystery. *"Gene, why are you involved in Zion Oil?"*, I asked. *"What's in it for you?"*

Of all the possible answers I had guessed at, his reply truly surprised me. Without hesitation he responded, *"An opportunity like this only comes along once in a lifetime."*

He knew when conditions were favorable for finding oil. In preparation for his successful thirty year career in the industry he had earned a Masters Degree from Massachusetts Institute of Technology, and was awarded the Sinclair Research Fellowship in Petroleum Economics. His education and career had prepared him to recognize the opportunity of a lifetime.

Gene had studied and understood the research compiled by Zion Oil. The oil man went on to explain that the geological and other data backing up the project were so convincing that the odds in favor of Zion being at the brink of discovering a massive oil reserve were too big to ignore. Gene was in it for the discovery. He didn't need the money (as President and CEO of Zion Oil, Gene earns a respectable salary...he doesn't actually take the salary; he's deferring payment until the company is pumping oil). He wasn't interested in the fame; he's saving that for the snipe circuit. The prophetic biblical side of it was fascinating to him and he approved of the company's charitable plans for profits, but those weren't his reasons for being involved. After a lifetime of great oil projects, this was the big one. Gene was willing to postpone the ease of a comfortable retirement and a few more snipe regattas to have a role in the oil discovery of a lifetime.

Speaking to the press, Gene keeps his excitement in check. Avoiding the details of the viability of the project due to SEC security regulations, he admits that Zion's Joseph project is a *"class A drillable prospect (with) reasonable chances of success...drillable by any international standards."* Meanwhile I can imagine his smile, betraying his public prudence...he's a man on the mission of a lifetime.

▶ **Glen Perry**, Zion's executive vice-president, also met John Brown in 1999. Glen's early experience as a petroleum engineer for some of the world's largest oil companies, including Exxon (now ExxonMobil) and Energy Reserves Group (now BHP), and manager of product development for a Swiss company doing business in the oilfields of the former Soviet Republic earned him recognition as one of the world's leading petroleum engineers. Glen was substantially involved in the exploration that produced Israel's huge off-shore natural gas discovery. It is the production from this huge natural gas reserve that now produces the fuel for much of Israel's electrical generation. As a world class petroleum engineer Glen was skeptical of John Brown's Bible based vision for oil in Israel. John, being on a mission from God, wasn't put off by Perry's skepticism. He commissioned Glen and Israeli geologist Dr. Eliezer Kashai to perform preliminary research *"below the foot of Asher"* and on the *"crown of the head of Joseph"*; the area in and around the current day Kibbutz Ma'anit. Glen Perry, doubtful of John Brown's story at their first meeting in 1999, has become a true believer. He has been with Zion Oil & Gas full time since April of 2000, currently serving as director and executive vice-president with the company, running their Israeli operations. When asked last year by the Israeli newspaper Haaretz about the vision of oil in Israel today he commented, *"People who say there is no oil in Israel speak out of ignorance. It's the biblical aspect that brought John (Brown), but our team has looked purely at the technical aspects of this project."*

►If you had to condense the history of Israeli oil exploration into a single name, **Eliezer Kashai** would rise to the top. Dr. Kashai (University of Sciences, Budapest, Hungary; M.A., Ph.D. Hebrew University, Jerusalem) has been at the beginning, middle, and end of every significant Israeli led oil exploration effort in the country since 1959. From 1959 to 1975 he served in progressively increasing roles, from senior geologist to chief geologist at Lapidoth, the Israeli government owned oil drilling entity. Oil Exploration Investment, Ltd. (OEIL), Israel's government owned oil exploration company employed Dr. Kashai first as chief geologist, then managing director. During his tenure as managing director of OEIL, Dr. Kashai was the official responsible for Israel's search for oil. After his *"retirement"* in 1987, Dr. Kashai served as an exploration consultant for the major private and government oil exploration efforts in the country, including the original geologic interpretation of Ma'anit, the well now being reopened by Zion Oil as part of the Joseph project. In his fifty years as a public and private oil geologist, Dr. Kashai has served as president of the Israeli Geological Society, and has published most of the geologic data relating to the country's potential oil reserves. Since October 2000 Dr. Kashai has served as Zion Oil's Vice-President of Israeli Oil Exploration.

Speaking in *"geologist"* for a recent video interview, Dr Kashai commented on the potential for a discovery at Ma'anit,

> *I mapped the reef...seismically and found that we have a barrier type reef between an open sea and a back lagoon within a supposedly high energy zone which will give us enough*

porosity and permeability to contain a large amount of petroleum...

Translated into *"layman"*, the Ma'anit well is sitting on top of an underground reef that, he believes, contains a tremendous amount of oil.

▶Consulting Geologist **Stephen Pierce** may not have written the book on oil in Israel but he did write what many consider the most comprehensive study and several technical articles on the subject. In 1980 the State of Israel commissioned Stephen (as an employee of Superior Oil Company) to conduct and publish a Basin Analysis Study of the country. In an exhaustive eighteen month study involving hundreds of kilometers of seismic tests, reprocessing hundreds more kilometers of existing test data, and analysis of data from the country's existing deep well Stephen was able to publish some very specific conclusions. The top three oil reserve prospects in the country were:

1. Off-shore, just off the coast of Haifa, the land known as the *"foot of Asher"*

2. The kibbutz Ma'anit area, where Zion is currently re-opening the Ma'anit 1 well.

3. A site in Zion's current license area know as the Joseph 1 prospect area.

The study was a seminal work in Israel's oil history, being the first single document to consolidate all existing information and scientifically and comprehensively identify Israel's greatest oil prospect areas.

In May of 2004 Stephen was commissioned to publish an additional independent study targeting the Ma'anit and Joseph license area. Confirming that geological evidence for oil reserves in the region is overwhelming; and noting that oil has recently been discovered just south of the license he praises Zion's prudent approach:

> *Zion has correctly adduced that there is a high probability of discovering a small commercial discovery and a correspondingly low probability of finding a large discovery. These conservative values are a welcome change from those provided by promoters that offer great rewards and severely underplay the risks.*

His conclusion to the study regarding Zion's license area is equally positive:

> *It is our opinion that Zion has reasonably evaluated the hydrocarbon potential of the Ma'anit – Joseph License and that they have analyzed and presented two drillable oil and gas exploration prospects consistent with the highest professional standards of the international oil industry. Given the risks that always accompany drilling oil wells, Zion has undertaken a better than normal due diligence in presenting the petroleum exploration prospects of the Ma'anit – Joseph License, Israel.*

Credited with perhaps the most significant industry appraisal regarding oil and Israel in the last fifty years, Stephen's article in the July 5, 2004 in the *Oil & Gas Journal* announced Israel's first substantial onshore oil find, Givot Olam's Meged 4 well, just south of Zion's license area.

Stephen Pierce, one of the world's highest regarded petroleum geologists; acclaimed for his early and recent work in Israel's oil future took it upon himself to contact Zion Oil & Gas, asking the company to consider taking him on as a team member.

Zion's miraculous résumé list continues to build as the search for Israel's oil nears its climax. Regardless of what critics have to say about Zion's reasons for searching for oil in Israel they fall silent when they consider the remarkable team of individuals that has been assembled for this mission.

The Joseph Project

The Ma'anit Joseph license consists of roughly 95,800 acres located between Tel Aviv and Haifa. Biblically speaking, the license area lies on the *"crown of the head of Joseph"* (Manasseh), just below the *"foot of Asher"*. Zion's first oil drilling project was to reopen and deepen an existing well in the area of the Kibbutz Ma'anit. The well, Ma'anit 1, was originally drilled to a depth of 7,651 feet in 1995 (with no substantial shows of oil or gas) before shutting down for lack of funds (after burning through about $5 million in exploration money). According to geologists, the well just isn't deep enough. Apparently, 7,651 feet deep only gets the well down to the late Jurassic era of the earth's history. If you remember your history (or your movies – *Jurassic Park*) this would be the time when dinosaurs ruled the earth.

Unfortunately for Israel, the earth their dinosaurs ruled wasn't favorable to storing a lot of oil. The geology (rocks and dirt) that represents the late Jurassic age in this part of Israel consisted of dolomitic limestone; all in all it was pretty close packed stuff; not much room for oil. What you really need to store a lot of oil (should you have the ingredients to make it) is a porous geologic structure, such as a reefal limestone deposit. Reefal limestone is full of holes. The difference between reefal limestone and the dolomitic limestone at the bottom of the original hole in Ma'anit 1 is like the difference between a block of Cheddar cheese and a block of Swiss cheese. The holes in the Swiss cheese make it a lot more porous than Cheddar. If you dunked a block of Swiss and a block of Cheddar into a bowl of olive oil, the holes in the Swiss would allow it to hold a lot more oil than the block of Cheddar. But of course, we're not talking about cheese and olive oil; we're talking about limestone and petroleum. Reefal limestone has a total porosity (storage capacity) up to twenty times greater than dolomitic limestone.

Fortunately for Israel, however, there was a time in the earth's history before the late Jurassic era. If you were able to travel to the 7,651 foot bottom of the original Ma'anit 1, then keep going down another 5,472 feet, the geology (rocks and dirt) you would be digging up would be from the Triassic and Permian eras. The Triassic and Permian eras aren't as popular as the Jurassic because there have been fewer movies made about them. But for the purposes of oil exploration the Triassic and Permian eras are extremely interesting. It seems that during this time Israel was covered by a shallow sea. The shallow sea produced a reef structures such as the Mohilla Formation in the late Triassic. The reef structures, made of limestone (reef + limestone = reefal limestone) have sufficient porosity to contain large amounts of oil. According to seismic studies, the depth (thickness) of the reef core below the Ma'anit well is estimated at thirteen hundred feet.

I learned this little fact during an interview with Zion's President and CEO Gene Soltero. He used the term *"vertical column"* to describe, in oil drilling terms, how much harvestable depth (the thickness of oil-bearing reef) a potential site contained. Thirteen hundred feet of *"vertical column"* seemed like a lot to me, but I had just learned the phrase and didn't have anything to compare it with. I asked the obvious, *"Is thirteen hundred feet of vertical column a lot?"*

He smiled at me like he'd just been asked, *"Is Christmas a big holiday?"* *"Here in Texas"*, Gene replied, *"we consider a well with thirty feet of vertical column to be a success."* Thirteen hundred feet of vertical column is apparently a lot of hole from which to pump oil.

In addition to a great place to store oil, like a reef structure (what oil folks call reservoir rock), a good oil prospect also needs, somewhere in its history, something from which to make oil. Oil, of course comes from ancient plants and animals (flora and fauna). These plants and animals die and eventually get buried by sediment; the sediment compresses and gets hot eventually becoming sedimentary rock (what oil folks call source rock). The warm shallow sea covering Israel during the Triassic era that produced the reef structure (the reservoir rock) also produced a lot of flora (plants) in the form of algae, or algal blooms (a lot of algae). According to Frank Stoakes, a world expert on reefs, this plant matter was compressed into the sediment (source rock), and eventually became crude oil and natural gas.

The last thing a good oil prospect needs is a seal; a lid to keep the oil in one place until it's pumped to the surface. Since oil and gas is lighter than water (in most cases) and since reservoir rocks are usually filled with water, the oil will rise, floating up over time through natural fractures in the subsurface rocks, eventually displacing the water in the reservoir rocks. What you need is a seal, or a cap above the reservoir to keep the oil and gas from migrating any further, so it will collect in the reservoir rock in sufficient quantities to make getting at it worth while. Remember all that tightly packed dolomitic limestone up in the Jurassic age? The shallower (Jurassic) subsurface structure that prevented any worthwhile oil and gas reservoirs turned out to be the perfect seal holding the deeper (Triassic and Permian) oil and gas reservoirs in place!

145

Bringing Oil to the Surface

There is only one rig in Israel capable of drilling a hole deep enough to reach the Triassic and Permian oil reserves. The Emsco 1500, owned by Israel's Lapidoth Drilling Company is the largest drilling rig in the country. Incidentally, this is the same rig that drilled the holes at Andy SoRelle's Atlit 1 and Givot Olam's Meged 4. On April 3, 2005 the Emsco rig stood center stage as Rabbi Yitsak Swartz pronounced his blessing at the public dedication of the reopening of Ma'anit 1, citing a passage from Deuteronomy,

> *They shall call the people unto the mountain; there they shall offer sacrifices of righteousness; for they shall suck of the abundance of the seas, and of treasures hid in the sand".*

(33:19)

I met Rabbi Swartz and his family at the Ma'anit well's dedication ceremony in Israel. His parents were a venerable Jewish couple; the father also a Rabbi wore a long beard and dressed in the traditional religious attire of his profession. I spoke slowly and simply to this old Israeli couple, hoping they would understand enough of my English to make conversation possible. It seems my communication concerns were unwarranted. The venerable Rabbi and his family had emigrated from El Paso, Texas to Israel several years previous. Evidently, the ties between Texas and Israel extend beyond the search for oil.

As of this writing the Lapidoth rig is under contract by Zion Oil & Gas and deepening the hole at Ma'anit 1 another 8,349 feet from its original depth of 7,651 feet, penetrating the Triassic era Mohilla Reef formation. Somewhere beyond 13,000 feet (a very deep well) Zion Oil & Gas should enter the remains of a 200 million year old sea.

This ancient sea, its massive reef structure once teeming with algae will see a second life in this age; transformed through millions of years of heat and pressure into a sea of petroleum.

The discovery of oil on the Ma'anit Joseph license will be the fulfillment of two promises; one to John Brown, a Michigan tool maker, simple enough in his belief to take God at his word twenty-five years earlier. And another made to Israel's children almost four-thousand years ago; that in the last days they would inherit the *"blessings of the deep"* and *"treasures in the sand"*.

CHAPTER 13

Israel Today

Slightly smaller than the state of New Jersey, most of Israel's land mass is desert. Virtually all economic and agricultural activity takes place in the central and northern parts of the country, inside of narrow borders; squeezed on the west by the Mediterranean Sea and on the east by the Palestinians, Jordan, and Syria.

---

[5] Source: UN Cartographic Section Map 3584 Rev 2

With as few natural resource options as she was given in her short history, Israel has made the most of them. In between wars and continual harassment by her enemy neighbors she has created an oasis out of desert and an economy from sand, sweat and blood.

The Economy

Israel's economy has taken a beating in recent years. Tourism, High-technology, diamond cutting, and agriculture are the mainstays of Israel's economy. Israel is known as *"The Holy Land"* for Christians, Jews, and Moslems around the world. Every year the country has counted on religious pilgrims and their tourist dollars as an economic staple. The threat of increased terrorism in Israel and around the world has all but killed Israeli tourism. High-technology and diamond cutting have suffered from a sharp decline of foreign investment, also a result of increasing terror activities. Agriculture is a bright spot in Israel's economy. Israel has successfully turned her deserts into gardens; feeding the nation and exporting much of its produce to European markets. Unfortunately, even a thriving agricultural industry, can't support all of Israel's economic needs. You can't grow a country or reverse a negative foreign trade balance on an economic diet of strawberries and pomegranates.

Since Binyamin Netanyahu became Finance Minister in 2000 Israel has begun sweeping changes to jump-start economic growth; like privatizing government owned companies in banking, telecommunications and oil exploration. Even these major changes in government spending and private investment, however, have not been enough to counter the economic hardships brought on by monstrous income taxes (up to 60%), and the sharp decline of tourism and foreign investment due to the increase in Palestinian terrorism.

Like every other modern society, petroleum plays a major role in Israeli everyday life. Since Israel imports virtually all of her oil, energy costs are expensive. According to a report in The Arutz Sheva Israel National News, the average Israeli family spends about 15% of their monthly income on fuel. Every dollar per barrel increase in the world's oil markets costs Israel $70 million in fuel costs per year.[6] With Israeli oil consumption at 100 million barrels per year, a major oil discovery inside of its borders would have a huge economic impact. No other imaginable windfall exists in Israel on the magnitude of a major oil discovery that would ensure her economic future.

Geo-Political Situation

Israel would be safer if she were energy independent. Currently her oil needs are met at the pleasure of her outside suppliers. If anything in world politics were to prevent or discourage Israel's outside supply base the country would shut down in days. World oil politics is, to a great extent, controlled by OPEC. OPEC is controlled by the Arab nations. The threat Israel's Arab neighbors hold over her and the rest of the world is oil. *"If you upset us, we will turn off the oil spigot. If you comply with our wishes we will provide you with oil."* Using world oil supply as a political weapon, with Israel in the cross-hairs, the Arabs could use their influence to slow Israel's foreign oil flow to a trickle.

As a part of the Camp David Peace accords the U.S. guaranteed Israel access to crude oil imports but its ability to make good on that promise in the event of a crisis is questionable. In the event of another world oil crisis, Israel could very well be on her own.

A major oil discovery in Israel wouldn't make the world stop buying oil from the Arabs and start buying it from

---

[6] "Oil Troubles in Israel", Arutz Sheva IsraelNationalNews.com, October 24, 2004

Israel. No huge relationship change with the US or European countries would bloom overnight. Deals have been made and infrastructures are already in place for oil supply to the developed world. But for Israel, it would spell economic security and political safety. Israel's oil independence would fulfill the prophecy in the Old Testament book of Deuteronomy, *"Israel then shall dwell in safety, alone."* (33:28)

Energy

Israel's energy comes from oil, natural gas, coal and solar. Of these energy sources all but solar rely on foreign imports. Coal accounts for most of Israel's electrical power generation fuel and satisfies about 17% of Israel's overall power consumption. Israel doesn't produce any coal; her entire supply is imported from Australia, South Africa, and Britain.

Today natural gas is the bright spot in Israel's energy future. Significant quantities of natural gas from offshore fields will make an impact on electrical production and heavy industry. This recently discovered source of energy means that existing oil fired electrical generation plants can be converted to burn cheap domestic natural gas rather than expensive imported oil. Currently only the Ashdod power generation plant is set up to produce electricity fueled solely from natural gas piped in from huge recently discovered gas fields off the Mediterranean coast near Ashkelon. Plans have been developed, however, to convert all oil burning electric plants to natural gas. In the north, the Atlit gas pipeline infrastructure is being installed now to power the Carmel electrical generation plant by 2007.

Israel has been the world leader in solar energy technology development. More than 80% of Israel's hot water comes from solar and all new home construction in the country is required to include solar hot water systems. A 100 mega-watt solar power generation station is planned for *"sometime in the future"* in the Negev Desert, but the hopes of solar technology making a practical impact beyond hot water is doubtful.

Currently Israel consumes about 270 thousand barrels of oil per day; about 72% of Israel's total energy consumption. Israel produces about 100 barrels of oil per day. To date Israel has produced about 18 million barrels of crude oil and the existing oil wells are about tapped out. Compared to the amount of oil she uses, it is safe to say current domestic oil production is non-existent. Israel imports virtually all of her oil from the former Soviet Republics, Mexico and Egypt.

Even with her miserable success in trying to find oil domestically, Israel encourages oil and gas exploration. The Israeli government energy effort, however, runs on a shoestring. About $250 million between 1975 and 1985 was spent in Israeli oil exploration, most of it from foreign investment. The government has privatized its oil companies, relying on outside investors to be the backbone of the country's oil and gas exploration efforts. The government negotiates exploration contracts and, as part of the deal shares access to all research and exploration data. At the expiration of the exploration contract this and any additional data, produced at the expense of foreign investors, is offered to new outside investors as Israel's contribution to further exploration efforts.

When it comes to oil and gas exploration, the government of Israel has done a very good job of getting a lot from outsiders with very little invested from the inside. To date almost all exploration costs have been paid by private companies, Israel shares in all of the exploration data and a portion of any potential profits, and can at her discretion redirect all production to domestic needs. In spite of the poor results a significant level of exploration has been accomplished. Over 420 exploration wells have been drilled and a good portion of the country is currently under some formed of exploration permit, license or lease.

The map below shows wells drilled in Israel's short history and areas currently under permit, license or lease.

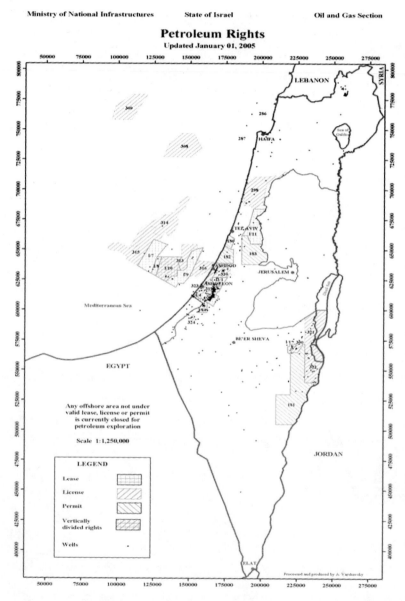

Problems

One of the significant problems in Israel's oil exploration efforts is that big oil companies, known as the *"Majors"* shy away from any public business dealings with the state of Israel due to their ongoing relationships with Arab countries. The Arab oil producing nations have made it clear to international companies that any business dealings with Israel would mean an automatic boycott from them. The *"Majors"* simply have too much invested in Arab oil production to risk disfavoring their suppliers by showing any business interest in Israel.

This threat of boycott has left the field in Israel open to small, independent oil exploration companies. The problem with the small independents is that they don't have the budget for extended exploration. Because of limited funds, exploration projects (and companies) often dry up with the first dry hole; and in the oil exploration business there are a lot of dry holes. Israel's difficult geology is another problem. According to seismic studies, the oil is deep and there are several problematic strata between the surface and potential reserves. Small independent companies with limited resources can risk going broke if they encounter extended drilling problems. Small independents often feel that they're better off simply putting their resources in other cheaper and easier to reach prospects.

The Israeli government has done little direct investment in finding oil domestically. They welcome outsiders who can pay their own way, but any exploration cost ends up being the responsibility of the outside investor. From Israel's perspective this is a fine approach; they enjoy the exploration efforts and possible future rewards at very little or no direct cost to the government. Unfortunately, the strategy of getting something for nothing hasn't produced significant oil deposits and it has a few problems that need to be considered:

1.   The Majors aren't interested (at least publicly). The world's big oil companies have the best chance for long term oil exploration success. If committed to a project, they have the financial ability to continue operations beyond a single dry hole or extended drilling difficulties.

2.   The small independent oil exploration companies lack the financial staying power in the event of dry holes or drilling problems. They also may lack the technical depth and production capability to follow through once a decent prospect has been identified.

3.   Incentive. The majors have no incentive to explore for oil in Israel. The bulk of their investments and profits are tied up in countries that are antagonistic toward Israel or anyone who befriends her. Why should they risk their current business in known terrain for potential future business in potentially difficult terrain? The small independents, for the most part, would rather invest their limited financial resources closer to home and in easier terrain. For a small independent in Houston, Texas there are prospects closer to home than Israel that can be tapped at lower initial cost.

Stakeholders

There are only three groups of potential oil explorers interested in Israel beyond a strict financial risk/benefit analysis. These three groups are the only people in the world who have an incentive that reaches beyond the current quarter's company balance sheet:

1.   **Israelis** – Domestic energy resources are of life and death importance to the people of Israel. Reliance on foreign oil currently strangles Israel's economy and endangers her security. Domestic oil production equal to or greater than

domestic consumption would create a financial boom greater than anything in Israel's history. The discovery of significant oil reserves would have far greater economic impact than any other potential industry boom on Israel's horizon, including tourism, high tech, and the diamond cutting industries combined.

Energy self-sufficiency for Israel would defang her Arab enemies...period. Foreign policy depends on oil. This is true of Israel, the U.S. and every other country on the globe. Decisions affecting every aspect of what one country does for, or to, another country are tainted by oil. Israel's foreign policy is held on a leash by the U. S and other countries partly because on her need for foreign oil. If anyone believes U.S. foreign policy isn't influenced by world oil supply he should become a better student of world political events over the last thirty years. Foreign policy, free from the need of foreign oil supply would change the face of Israel's status in the world, both among her friends and enemies.

2.   **Jews** – Jews around the world have been a primary source of supply for the State of Israel since before her birth on May 14, 1948. World Jewry supplies Israel with immigrants to fill the country's human resource needs, and provides financial resources in the form of charitable giving, direct business investment, technology, and tourism. Jews around the world are connected to Israel and are intensely interested in her health and survival in the future. Jews world wide should be profoundly interested in Israel's oil independence.

3.   **Christians** – Jews don't necessarily claim Christians as spiritual brothers. Christians do, however, claim Jews. Christians believe that the Jews are God's chosen people. According to the analogy of an olive tree in the New Testament book of Romans, Israel is the true root and Gentile Christians are merely grafted in shoots from a wild olive.

> *"If some branches have been broken off, and you, though a wild olive shoot, have been grafted in among the others and now share in the nourishing sap from the olive root, do not boast over those branches. If you do, consider this: You do not support the root, but the root supports you."*
>
> (Romans 11:17-18 NIV)

Israel is the political extension of the Jewish people; as an independent state she represents the Jews as a people. Christians should be interested in the health and survival of Israel as an independent state to the extent they identify with the Jews as God's chosen people.

The Israeli Perspective

The Israelis, forced to be warriors from their birth, are a people who truly desire peace. Surrounded by enemies, they defend themselves and wish for a peace with neighbors that know only conflict. A man I met in Israel recently showed us the country's historical treasures and recent accomplishments. Proud of his people and their mission of building a thriving country from a wilderness in just fifty years, he spoke of future possibilities that today are still a dream. As we traveled through Israel's lush northern countryside he mused aloud:

> *If only we could reach a peace with our neighbors, we could prosper together. First we would plant trees, and forests could grow in the desert of our neighbors as they do now in Israel. We could make fertile ground in the desert in just a few years, as we've done in Israel.*

For a man who was born into war, whose parents survived Hitler's holocaust death camps, who as a child learned how to run from the school bus to the shelter of rock outcroppings when the Syrian shells rained down from the Golan Heights, I heard a dream of peace. What I didn't hear in his dialogue was hatred. I didn't hear forgiveness or forgetfulness, but neither did I hear hatred. Whether peace between Arab and Jew is possible only God knows. That Israelis deeply desire to live in peace is evident in their eyes, in their language, and in their dreams for the country.

Jews vs. Christians

Israeli Jews view American evangelical Christians with skepticism. They are suspicious of evangelical Christians' motives; believing them to have their own agenda. Most Israeli Jews believe Christians' interest in Israel is to either proselytize the people (convert Jews to Christianity) or to bring about the battle of Armageddon in order to usher in the return of the Messiah. Incredibly, a popular belief among some Israeli Jews is that Christians are helping Israel in order to get the world's Jews back to the Holy Land so that they may be killed in the battle of Armageddon. Christians I've shared this perception with are shocked that a misconception this far from their beliefs exists in Israel.

Many religious Jewish Zionists are open to aid from American evangelical Christians because of the shared belief that all of Israel (including Gaza and the West Bank) rightfully belongs to the Jews. Jewish Zionists, however, see assistance from American Christians as a marriage of convenience. They are not tickled over their new found allies in the struggle for their homeland, but beggars can't be choosers; and American evangelical Christians seem to be the only non-Jewish friends to come forward. American evangelical Christians do have their own agenda; and it's not to round up the world's Jews for the last battle. American evangelicals believe that the Jews, particularly Jews in Israel will be saved physically and spiritually in the last days.

Most Zionist Jews look sideways at Gentiles, even those trying to help. The belief that Christians have their own motives for their apparent friendship has been demonstrated, to the injury of Jews, throughout history. Among Jews, however, there does exist the concept of a *"righteous Gentile"*. These are Gentiles who truly seek to help the Jews without any ulterior motives. In Israel's history, Lord Wingate (Wingate Center) and Lawrence Oliphant (Scottish writer) are examples of *"righteous Gentiles"*. According to Israeli attorney Philip Mandelker, John Brown of Zion Oil & Gas is a *"righteous Gentile"*. He may not be the only Christian oil prospector to be regarded so highly by Israelis, but the list of *"righteous Gentiles"* isn't a long one.

The core difference between religious Jews and evangelical Christians is that the Jews do not believe that Jesus Christ was and is the Messiah. Jews are waiting for the Messiah to come; Christians are waiting for the Messiah to return. Mendy Gunda, an Israeli friend and tour guide illustrates this difference of opinion with a joke for his Christian clientele. *"What's the first question a Jew will ask the Messiah when he comes?"* The answer: *"Is this your first visit to the Holy Land?"*

The idea of the coming Messiah, however, is very real in the hearts of Zionist Jews. Jewish settlers in the Palestinian Gaza Strip are being relocated to Israeli land as part of the Israeli/Palestinian *"Roadmap to Peace"*. When interviewed, one Zionist settler who was losing his home in the Gaza community his people built was philosophic in his larger view of the situation, *"The train is going into a tunnel...But it is moving forward. Every day brings us closer to the days of the Messiah."*[7]

---

[7] "Settlers Ignore Gaza Countdown", Chicago Tribune April 22, 2005

The Christian Perspective

There are two reasons for evangelical Christians to be pro-Israel. The first is that evangelical Christians believe the Jews are God's chosen people. The State of Israel is the God promised homeland of the Jews. Honoring, defending, and supporting Israel, from a Christian perspective, honors God.

According to the New Testament Gentile Christians are *"grafted in"* to God's family, like adopted children. The Jews (Israel) are God's chosen people or *"chosen children"*. Gentile Christians believe that God's chosen people, whether they accept Jesus as Messiah or not, are to be held in special regard.

The New Testament also teaches that in the end times (the period just before Christ returns to establish his kingdom on earth) that Israel will return to her land and prosper. Ultimately the Messiah will return and Israel will be saved physically and spiritually as a part of Christ's reign on earth and of his eternal kingdom.

The Arab Perspective

In their view, Arabs have received the short end of the stick from the Jews since the day they were born. Abraham, the father of the both Ishmael (from whom the Arabs descend) and Isaac (from whom the Jews descend) forsook tradition by giving Ishmael's rights and blessing as first born son to Isaac. Isaac's oldest son Esau also lost out at the hands of his younger brother Jacob. By bribes and treachery, Jacob stole Esau's birthright and blessing. Esau moved south, bereft of his blessing as first-born, to a desert land eventually becoming his namesake *"Edom"* (Esau and Edom both mean *"red"*). The Arab nations descend from Ishmael and Esau. The Jews descend from Isaac and Jacob (Israel). From the Arab perspective, Jews have been cheating Arabs out of their birthright and blessing since the beginning.

God's perspective, however, prevails in the long run. He chooses who he chooses, regardless of who was first-born. God doesn't answer to man in His decision making process. In choosing Isaac and Jacob, however, He did not completely bankrupt Ishmael and Esau. God remembered the complaint of Ishmael's mother Hagar and promised,

And as for Ishmael, I have heard: Behold, I have blessed him, and will make him fruitful, and will multiply him exceedingly; twelve princes shall he beget, and I will make him a great nation.

(Genesis 17:20)

Esau didn't escape God's blessing either. When he complained to his father Isaac that little brother Jacob had stolen the blessing rightly belonging to him, Isaac produced an additional blessing for Esau,

...Behold, thy dwelling shall be the fatness of the earth, and of the dew of heaven from above; And by thy sword shalt thou live, and shalt serve thy brother; and it shall come to pass when thou shalt have the dominion, that thou shalt break his yoke from off thy neck.

(Genesis 27:39-40)

Esau founded Edom; today the country of Saudi Arabia. The word *"fatness"* in Esau's blessing above is the same ancient Hebrew word for oil. The promise that, *"thy dwelling shall be the fatness* (oil) *of the earth"* has been abundantly fulfilled in present day Saudi Arabia.

God didn't neglect His promises of nationhood and dominion to Ishmael and Esau. From the 5th century AD, when the religion of Islam was establish to today the Arab nations have had nearly complete control of the Middle East. Arab nations today control about 99% of the land mass in the

Middle East and most of the world's proven oil reserves. With all of this, they still hold a powerful grudge against the children of Isaac and Jacob. Their hatred for the people of Israel is endemic. The Arab world sees Israel as a usurper; a nation that occupies territory rightly belonging to the sons of Ishmael and Esau. The sworn oath to *"drive Israel into the sea"* is their single cure for this four thousand year old resentment. Only then, will they feel that ancient wrongs have been put right.

News of a vast oil reserve discovered in the land of Israel would infuriate the Arab world for several reasons. First, since Israelis are regarded as trespassers and usurpers, any oil found in Israel would be viewed as the property of the Arab world by ancient right. The people of Israel benefiting from oil found in the land of Israel (which Arabs believe rightly belongs to them) is equivalent to Israelis stealing Arab oil.

Secondly, Arab legitimacy in the modern world comes from oil. Arabs enjoy their current level of importance and regard in the world because of their oil reserves. This may not be a popular statement but it's a true one. Israel, their birth enemy, suddenly becoming oil rich would insult the Arab world as a blow to their single source of status among the nations.

Thirdly, oil independence would make Israel stronger; economically and militarily. The idea of an economically and militarily strong Israel flies in the face of Arab domination in the region. A weak enemy is better than a strong one any day. Israel's Arab enemies have been pitifully inefficient in destroying her in the last fifty years; chances for an Arab victory in the future would be greatly diminished if Israel were energy self-sufficient and economically secure.

Fourthly, Israel having sufficient production to export oil could significantly reduce the cartel power OPEC enjoys today. To Arabs, the idea of Israel exporting oil is even more heinous than her oil self-sufficiency.

Not Enemies (sort of)

Not every Arab nation is sworn enemies with Israel. As a result of a February 2005 Mid-East Peace Summit in Egypt, Jordan and Egypt have reestablished diplomatic relations with Israel. This warming came as a result of the renewed promise of peace between Israel and the Palestinians. Egypt and Jordan are currently the only two Arab countries having peace treaties with Israel.

Turkey is another exception. Although not Arab, Turkey is a Moslem country, throughout Israel's 50 year history Turkey has, to a great extent, maintained positive diplomatic relations.

The Boycott

The Arab boycott of Israel has been a part of its history since the country's birth in 1948. The Arab League (council of Arab nations) officially boycotted Israel; refusing to do business with Israel or any third country firms that have business dealings with Israel. The Arab countries know that they can use their oil trade with third parties as a powerful economic weapon against Israel. In 1978 the U.S. passed a law forbidding any U.S. company from participating with or agreeing to the boycott; but many other countries complied with Arab demands.

In spite of UN restrictions in Iraq's *"Oil for Food"* program after the first Gulf War, Iraq continued to coerce foreign business partners into the boycott. In 2004 U.S. investigators obtained copies of Iraqi contracts with Russian and Egyptian food and medicine suppliers pledging not to do business with Israel or ship product to Iraq through Israel. The Iraqi contract reinforces this pledge.

> *We hereby confirm our commitment and pledge not to deal with Israel. So that in the event of any infringement of this condition the Iraqi party will definitely cancel the contract and stop any future dealing with our firm.*[8]

Most European countries have drafted laws against this kind of discrimination; but for some, their *"business is business"* mentality creates paths around anti-discrimination laws. France, who conducted considerable business with Iraq and today trades heavily with other Arab nations, has negotiated *"boycott"* language into their contracts, seemingly complying with the Arab boycott and European law.

The Moslem World

The Arab world is overwhelmingly Moslem. That is, the religion of the Arab world is Islam; so much so that the terms *"Arab World"* and *"Moslem World"* are used in conversation interchangeably. The Moslem world encompasses more than the Arab world, but the Arab nations are the controlling entities in the world of Islam. Muslim's, almost completely, share the Arabs' hostility toward the Jews. Iran's (Persian, not Arab) Ayatollah Ali Khamenei did his bit for the continued hatred of Israel and the U.S. by proposing a new Middle East oil policy to a crowd of his countrymen while they chanted *"Death to Israel and America."*[9] His idea for Middle East oil policy was simple,

---

[8] "Baghdad Butcher's Oil Biz Slap at Israel", New York Post, October 16, 2004

[9] "Iranian Urges Muslims to Use Oil as a Weapon", New York Times, April 6, 2002

"The oil belongs to the (Muslim) people and can be used as a weapon against the West and those who support the Savage regime of Israel." According to Ayatollah Khamenei's fundamentalist Muslim theology, Israel is the *"Little Satan"* and America is the *"Big Satan"*. If the world is to be set right, the followers of Allah need to rid it of both *"Satan"* twins. Peace in the Middle East, as far as the fundamentalist Moslem world is concerned, involves the destruction and eradication of the State of Israel.

The Saudis, viewed as moderates and friends of the U.S., killed Ayatollah Khamenei's proposal to turn off the oil supply. However, Saudi Arabia, the world's largest oil producer and exporter and the most powerful voice in the Arab nations is in a tenuous position. OPEC's most powerful member is a one commodity economy. The commodity, of course is oil. Even though Saudi Arabia has always played the part of moderate and friend of U.S. policy in the Arab world, its autocratic rulers continually walk the tight rope between their Western customers and their increasing anti-West population. For all the oil money injected into it, the Saudi economy is anything but robust. Unemployment is high and the jobs that do exist are usually dead-end bureaucratic busywork. The young Saudi population is being wooed heavily by Moslem fundamentalists encouraging a break with the West. Any change in the Saudi's standard of living stemming from less demand or lower prices for its only source of income could tip the scales in favor of the radical population. The next time radical fundamentalist Moslem leaders demand an end to Western oil supply, the Saudi's may not be able to prevent the idea from becoming reality.

The Palestinian Problem

"Invisible" would be an apt description for the Arab Oil States in the latest attempts to ensure a lasting peace between Israel and the Palestinians. They've been invisible

in the peace process, but not invisible altogether. Iran is the major financer of Palestinian terrorism and the Arab States have never explicitly said that peace between Israel and the Palestinians would be a good thing. Secretly (or not so secretly) they look forward to continued conflict in the area, hoping it will lead to the eventual downfall of the Jewish state. If the millions of dollars pumped into the Palestinian terror network by Iran and other Arab States were given to assist the Palestinians in building homes, schools and businesses rather than destroy both Palestinian and Jewish lives, the possibility of a Palestinian State becoming a reality would be much greater today.

The Palestinian Perspective

The Palestinian State is to be the independent homeland for Arab people living in the land of Palestine prior to the founding of the nation of Israel. The *"Palestinian Authority"* was set up as a pre-Palestine governing body; gaining status to *"independent country"*, the world hoped, by 2005. The birth of the Palestinian State is not on track. The current plan for Middle East peace, put together by the U.S., the European Union, Russia, and the U.N., called the *"Road Map"* to peace is to be achieved in phases, ultimately leading to an independent Palestinian State. Israel and the Palestinian Authority are still in phase one; and it isn't going well.

In Phase One of the plan, Palestinians are supposed to halt all terror activities. Since the *"Road Map"* was laid out, terrorist attacks have increased, not halted or even decreased. With the death of Yasser Arafat, in many eyes the primary nurturer of Palestinian terrorism, hope sprang up for a Palestinian effort at the peace plan. Israel, as their part in the peace process was to stop building settlements in Palestinian territories and begin dismantling existing settlements. Israeli settlement building inside Palestinian territory has increased since the peace plan was laid out. In spite of the recent campaign pulling Israeli settlers out of the Gaza Strip (Palestinian territory), settlement building in the Palestinian West Bank has continued as scheduled. The *"Road Map"* has hit a road block. Neither side will engage in Phase One without proof that the other is simultaneously fulfilling their half of the bargain. Neither side is making promises that they will comply, whether the other side fulfills their end or not. From whoever's perspective it's viewed, the Israeli/Palestinian *"Road Map"* to peace has taken a detour.

Palestinian terrorism continues to increase in spite of the attempted peace process. Incidents of attacks from terrorist groups went up in 2004 from the year before. Due to Israeli Defense Forces checkpoints and the disputed security wall between Israel and the West Bank, however, Israeli fatalities and injuries have gone down. Regardless of the political uproar the security wall and IDF checkpoints have caused, these two measures have saved Israeli civilian lives. An upswing in the relatively ineffective mortar and Kassam rocket attacks from inside Palestinian territory and the marked decrease of more deadly suicide bombings is proof that Israeli measures to limit terrorists access has been successful.

There is a school of thought that says if a vast oil deposit was discovered in the land that the resulting prosperity would lead to a lasting peace between Palestinians and Israel. The idea being that neither party could afford to be at war against the other with such a treasure at stake. A peace between Palestinians and Israelis driven by mutual oil wealth sounds like a great idea. Unfortunately, the mutual animosity between the two parties isn't driven by who gets dibs over valuable mineral resources. The resource is the land itself. As long as Israel exists in the land, Palestinians, like their Arab brothers, will continue to regard the Jews as invaders. The State of Israel, of course, isn't going anywhere. Not only is Israel committed to staying in the land rightfully apportioned to them by the League of Nations in

1947; many in Israel are committed to occupy the land rightly apportioned to them by God three thousand years ago. The land apportioned to them by God includes the Palestinian territory. Israel's Prime Minister makes no bones about it. Israel is not going to make any unilateral effort to ensure the reality of an independent Palestinian state.

The World's Perspective

Depending on which U.S. Government Department of Energy report you read, current world oil production is about 80 million barrels per day. Daily world oil consumption is 80 millions barrels, matching production. The world burns as much oil as it produces. Demand, however, is estimated to nearly double by the year 2025. Proven world oil reserves today are estimated at just under 1.28 billion barrels. At the present growth rate of demand with the current proven reserves, the world's oil fields should be going dry in about twenty-five years.

Greatest Oil Reserves by Country, 2003

2002 rank	Country	2003 proved reserves (billion barrels)
1.	Saudi Arabia	261.7
2.	Iraq	115.0
3.	Iran	100.1
4.	Kuwait	98.9
5.	United Arab Emirates	63.0
6.	Russia	58.8
7.	Venezuela	53.1
8.	Nigeria	32.0
9.	Libya	30.0
10.	China	23.7

NOTES: Figures for Russia are "explored reserves," which are understood to be proved plus some probable. All other figures are proved reserves recoverable with present technology and prices.

Source: World Oil. Vol. 224, No. 8 (Aug. 2003). From: U.S. Energy Information Administration, International Energy Annual 2002 (March–June 2004).

Top World Oil Producers, Exporters, Consumers, and Importers, 2003

(millions of barrels per day)

Producers[1]	Total oil production	Exporters[2]	Net oil exports	Consumers[3]	Total oil consumption	Importers[4]	Net oil imports
1. *Saudi Arabia*	9.95	1. *Saudi Arabia*	8.38	1. United States	20.0	1. United States	11.1
2. United States	8.84	2. Russia	5.81	2. China	5.6	2. Japan	5.3
3. Russia	8.44	3. Norway	3.02	3. Japan	5.4	3. Germany	2.5
4. *Iran*	3.87	4. *Iran*	2.48	4. Germany	2.6	4. South Korea	2.2
5. Mexico	3.79	5. *United Arab Emirates*	2.29	5. Russia	2.6	5. China	2.0
6. China	3.54	6. *Venezuela*	2.23	6. India	2.2	6. France	2.0
7. Norway	3.27	7. *Kuwait*	2.00	7. South Korea	2.2	7. Italy	1.7
8. Canada	3.11	8. *Nigeria*	1.93	8. Canada	2.2	8. Spain	1.5
9. *United Arab Emirates*	2.66	9. Mexico	1.74	9. Brazil	2.1	9. India	1.4
10. *Venezuela*	2.58	10. *Algeria*	1.64	10. France	2.1		
11. United Kingdom	2.39	11. *Libya*	1.25	10. Mexico	2.1		
12. *Kuwait*	2.32						
13. *Nigeria*	2.25						

NOTE: OPEC members in italics.

1. Table includes all countries with total oil production exceeding 2 million barrels per day in 2002. Includes crude oil, natural gas liquids, condensate, refinery gain, and other liquids.
2. Includes all countries with net exports exceeding 1 million barrels per day in 2002.
3. Includes all countries that consumed more than 2 million barrels per day in 2002.
4. Includes all countries that imported more than 1 million barrels per day in 2002.
Source: Energy Information Administration (EIA). www.eia.doe.gov/emev/topworldtables1_2.html

Russia

As allies with the U. S. against Germany during World War II the Soviet Union was obligated to support the 1947 UN Partition of Palestine Resolution and recognize Israel as an independent State in 1948. The relationship between the USSR and Israel declined rapidly after that. The Soviets soon changed allegiance and began backing Egypt and Syria in the Middle East. The Soviets were also among the first to begin supplying the PLO (Palestinian Liberation Organization) with military hardware to use against Israel.

In the mid-1980's the Soviets tried a warming tactic in an effort to counter-balance the strong U.S relationship with Israel and to be seen as a *"player"* in the Middle-East peace process. They hosted their own *"peace summit"* in Helsinki in an effort to re-establish relations with Israel. Part of the deal they were seeking was increased access to Israel, both in diplomatic (spy) venues and travel of Soviet citizens to Israel. They were also interested in Soviet property in Israel, namely that of the Russian Orthodox Church.

Israel had its own interests in the apparent warm front coming down from Russia. The Soviets possessed two assets of great value to Israel. The USSR was home to a huge population of Jews and many of these Jews would immigrate to Israel if given the opportunity. Israel wanted a much freer immigration policy for Jews coming from Soviet States. Another asset Israel couldn't turn down was oil. Soviet oil fields were pumping about 12 million barrels a day in 1986. Russian oil supply was fat, cheap and close to Israel. Despite its history of backing her enemies Israel saw the USSR as a promising source for her oil needs. Today Israel imports the majority of her oil from the former Soviet Union – Russia and the Caspian region (Kazakhstan, Turkmenistan, etc.).

Russia is determined to take a greater role in Israel's future. Other than the U.S., Russia is the only single country entity with an active role in the Israel/Palestinian *"Road Map"* to peace. Member powers of the *"Quartet"*, the body responsible for creating and ensuring the *"Road Map"* peace plan include the U.S., Russia, the European Union, and the U.N. Russian president Vladimir Putin is stepping to the forefront by hosting *"Quartet"* meetings and the next Middle East peace conference in Moscow. Russia has also pushed for a closer relationship with Israel in the areas of Israel's large Russian speaking population and anti-terrorism. With all its feints toward an Israeli/Palestinian peace Russia continues, however, to back the Palestinian cause and slander Israel through front organizations such as the World Peace Council.[10]

Russia and her former satellite states now supply Israel with 80% of its imported oil. If Israel were to suddenly discover reserves sufficient to become oil independent, the former Soviet States would lose a very important customer. If Israel were to stop buying oil, Russia's reasons for positive relations would diminish. With an increasing Moslem foothold in the former Soviet States, Russia could easily return to the side of *"old friends"* (war materiel customers) in the Middle East.

Current proven oil reserves in Russia and the former Soviet states are 79.2 billion barrels. Today these states produce about 11.3 million barrels per day. Following the expected increase in demand and assuming production will increase to meet demand, the former Soviet states should run out of oil by 2020.

Western Europe

As a group, Western Europe is pretty straight forward and pragmatic when it comes to Israel. It doesn't carry the religious zeal or political hatred of the Arab world and it lacks any spiritual or cosmic reason to support Israel. Simply put, Europe wants what it wants for its own purposes and if working with Israel gets it what it wants, it's ready to be friends. If being friends with Israel prevents it from getting what it wants, then Israel is out of the picture and new friends (OPEC) are in. Europe does have Jewish and Christian populations that are pro-Israel and Moslem populations that are pro-Arab; but neither group necessarily affects foreign policy. Recent Islamic terrorism, unfortunately, has managed to steer the ship of foreign

---

[10] "Putin Due in Israel on Historic Visit", Associated Press, April 27, 2005

policy in some European countries. Europe's dual personality is born from and fueled by commercial interests. The region depends heavily on Arab oil and they will do nothing politically to upset that supply. Europe demonstrated during the days leading to the fall of Iraq that alienating Israel and the U.S. if necessary would not be too high a price to pay to preserve their established oil for *"anything you want"* contract with OPEC nations. On the other hand, about 40% of Israeli foreign trade, in the form of agricultural products and high-tech goes to Western Europe. Western Europe isn't bound by any moral or religious restrictions concerning the Arabs or the Israelis; just give them what they want and they'll put on the face required for the day.

An oil discovery in Israel sufficient for export to European markets may increase *"warm feelings"* toward Israel. On the other hand, Arab nations remain Europe's largest oil supplier. In the event of a major oil discovery in Israel it will be interesting to see where Europe finds its best deal and its closest ally.

China and the Far East

There is a dragon asleep in the backyard and its name is China. She's been asleep for a long time, but now she is beginning to wake; and when she's awake and active the entire world will feel her hot breath on its neck. China is the largest single emerging market the world has ever seen. Leading the pack of Asian countries, including India and South Korea, China and her neighbors combined currently consume about 75% of the energy consumed in North America (U.S., Canada, and Mexico) By 2025 China and her neighbors will consume nearly 30% more total energy than North America. Asia will feed her exploding energy requirements from some source. How, where, and what strings may be attached to Asia's oil supply are anyone's guess. One thing is certain, however, Asia, with China leading, will eclipse every other oil consumer in the world.

The US Perspective

The U.S. imports 13 million barrels of oil per day; about 60% of its total consumption. 20% of that comes from Arab nations in the Persian Gulf. According to Red Caveny,[11] the President and CEO of the American Petroleum institute, America's demand for energy will increase significantly over the next twenty years. Quoting Department of Energy forecasts in his State of the Energy Industry 2005 address he gives the numbers the U.S. can expect through 2025:

- Real GDP will increase by 95 percent

- Population will increase by 20 percent

- Total energy consumption will increase by 36 percent

- Petroleum demand will increase by 39 percent

- Natural gas demand will increase by 40 percent

- Coal demand will increase by 34 percent

- Electricity consumption will increase by 50 percent

Caveny went on to say that America's greatest energy problem was the lack of any comprehensive plan for the future. The net effect, according to Caveny, of the current U.S. energy policy is to decrease reliance on domestic sources and increase dependence of foreign imports. This means that over the next twenty years America's reliance on foreign oil will increase exponentially. Caveny goes on to say,

---

[11] "State of the Energy Industry 2005, Petroleum Issues", American Petroleum Institute, January 18, 2005

We cannot discuss the challenge of meeting the growing U.S. energy demand without first understanding the global energy situation. In the world of energy, the U.S. must operate in a global market. What others do in that market matters greatly.

Israeli oil independence probably wouldn't have a profound effect on America's energy future. The U.S. is by far, the world's largest user and importer of oil. No single oil exporting country, including Saudi Arabia, could supply U.S. consumption. At a rate 21 million barrels per day, U.S. consumption matches the total daily output from the Persian Gulf nations.

U.S foreign policy toward Israel addresses Israel's oil supply, not her potential surplus. For better or worse, current U.S. foreign policy ensures Israeli oil supply. The United States, in a 1975 *"memorandum of understanding"* with Israel, guaranteed the supply of Israel's oil needs in the event of a crisis, even if it means reducing America's oil supply.[12] The U.S. and Israel have also signed an energy cooperation agreement in February of 2000 that promises teamwork in the areas of natural gas, coal, solar technology, and electrical generation.[13]

The U.S., however, learned its lesson during the first Arab oil embargo. Never again will it enact any foreign policy without first considering how the Arab world will react. The Arab world has become very much a part of America's foreign policy decision making. Between America's loyalties to Israel and its energy threat from the Arabs, it walks a tightrope, that falling from, wherever it landed would be devastating.

---

[12] "Israel's pipe dream: getting oil from Iraq." The St. Petersburg Times, August 15, 2004

[13] "Israel's ongoing foreign energy dependence." UPI Perspective, August 11, 2004

As far as American opinion regarding Israel and Middle East peace goes, it's as varied as the backgrounds this country's people hail from. In a May 17, 2001 letter to the editor titled *"Safer to Bomb Civilians"* in The Houston Chronicle Art Milstein spoke for many Americans when he voiced his frustration over the conflict between Israelis and Palestinians.

> *Like any thinking person I'm appalled at what's happening in Gaza and the West Bank. I don't believe Ariel Sharon's visit caused it – it was too well organized and just waiting to happen.*

> *And I feel disgusted by the world's media handling of the news. Rocks can kill and maim; are soldiers supposed to throw rocks back?*

> *It's stupid to throw rocks and try to burn people who carry guns. Bombing a busload of civilians or a market is safer.*

> *I feel for the plight of Palestinians: in 50 years, their Arab "brothers" have offered them only guns, not homes.*

> *If Israel had oil, it would be safer. And don't be misled: When push comes to shove, the world will feel Jews are cheaper than oil. I wouldn't blame God if he gave up on us all.*

CHAPTER 14

Significance

Ishmael, Isaac, Jacob and Esau

Ishmael and Isaac, in their day, viewed their relative positions and destinies from their unique individual and historic perspectives. Ishmael was Abraham's oldest son, born to him by Hagar, his wife's servant. By ancient custom the first born son deserved his father's blessing and birthright. Isaac, Abraham's second son, born to him by his wife Sarah was God's promised child. By God's choice, Isaac was given the birthright and blessing, belonging by custom to Ishmael. This created an enmity between Ishmael and Isaac, but the idea that someday their descendents would be warring nations and the world's focus would rest on their petroleum reserves was outside of their comprehension - beyond their perspective.

Esau and Jacob, in their day, viewed their relative positions and destinies from their unique individual and historic positions. Twins, sons of the same father and mother, born on the same day; their issues and circumstances were not the same as those of their father Isaac or Uncle Ishmael. Esau and Jacob had their own destinies, as God prophesied to Rebekah their mother,

> ...*Two nations are in thy womb, and two manner of people shall be separated from thy bowels; and the one people shall be stronger than the other people; and the elder shall serve the younger.*

(Genesis 25:23)

Esau the oldest, long on brawn and short on brain, traded his birthright to his twin brother Jacob for a bowl of soup. Later, when the boys were men and father Isaac was old and nearing death, Jacob bested his brother again by obtaining their father's blessing, reserved for the first-born, by deceit. Tricking his brother and father, Jacob, whose name literally means *"grabber"*, had grabbed the birthright and blessing meant for Esau. Jacob and Esau, like their father and uncle, viewed their circumstances from ground level. Like their father and uncle, that they would become the progenitors to warring nations and inheritors of the world's petroleum reserves was outside of their ability to comprehend – beyond their perspective.

Today this ancient family feud is about a lot more than sheep, goats, camels and the family tent. Ishmael, Isaac, Esau, and Jacob are all just names from history - dead forefathers. Nations have risen from men and petroleum oil has replaced olive oil as a universal commodity. The old enmity between these brothers still exists but the stakes have gone up. Today Israel and the Arab nations, if not at open war, are at least circling in a wary detent. The ongoing terror campaign waged against Israel is testimony that war, not peace, is always lying just beneath the surface. The sons of Jacob (Israel) are still called "grabbers" by their Arab relatives. The sons of Esau are still wanting their birthright and blessing back.   Unfortunately, the perspective hasn't changed much. The sons of Jacob and Esau, Isaac and Ishmael are only seeing from ground level.

Perspective

Perspective is the view of an object relative to the position of the viewer. The closer the viewer is to an object the more restricted his view is of the entire object. As the viewer backs away from the object his view, his perspective, grows so that he sees the object and the space surrounding it more clearly.

I have a large map of the world hanging on my office wall.

▶ **If I place my nose** on the map's surface, with Los Angeles as ground zero, my perspective of the map and the world is extremely limited. In fact I can't even see Los Angeles; everything's a blur.

▶ **If I pull my nose six inches away** from the wall my vision begins to clear. At six inches, my eyes can't perfectly focus but I can read some print on the map. I see Los Angeles and I can read the names of the cities surrounding Los Angeles. In my peripheral vision I can even vaguely make out parts of Canada to the north, Mexico to the south and the blue of oceans on either side.

▶ **Pulling my face twelve inches away** from the wall I can read the names of the cities, states and provinces of North America clearly. I see that the Pacific Ocean borders North America on the west and the Atlantic borders it on the east. In my peripheral vision I can see other continents on either side where the oceans end.

▶ **From three feet away** the world comes into view; with North America in the center (thanks to Rand McNally). I can see Africa and Europe, to the east of North America. Russia, Asia and Australia lie to the west of center. I can see how the countries are placed within continents, their relative proximity to neighbors and relative distance from lands far away.

▶ **At six feet** I can view the entire map at a glance. I see how Russia and China, sliced in half by the map's right border, continue on the left from where they were bisected. From six feet I can still read the names of the countries and continents printed on the map, but the names of cities are too small for me to make out. By the latitudinal and longitudinal lines growing outward as they travel away from the equator I understand that the map displays distance in smaller increments close to the equator, increasing in size as it travels away from the equator. This makes Greenland, in the far north appear slightly larger than South America in the center, when in reality South America is about nine time the size of Greenland. I remember then that the earth is a globe, not flat like the map and that these growing distances are a cartographer's tool to display a round globe on a flat wall. At six feet I can finally see the world for what it is and understand the map in its full view. At this distance I also realize that the map is not the only object in the room. In my periphery I can see my desk to the left of the map and bookshelves to the right; beyond the desk I even catch a glimpse of my office window which reveals the world outside.

By backing slowly away from the map my vision came into focus. As I continued to back away I gained perspective; first seeing Los Angeles clearly, then North America, then the world, and finally the map itself. I realized that Los Angeles wasn't the only object on the map, nor was North America. The entire world was included. I realized also that the map was not the world, but just the mapmaker's depiction of the world. The mapmaker created the map to be viewed at a distance of about six feet, so that men, when they looked upon the map gained a perspective of the world.

The Lesson

With my nose on the map everything is a blur. At six inches I can see only what is in front of my face, maybe the city in which I live but that's about all. At twelve inches I can see the country I live in and its immediate neighbors but the rest of the world is unclear in the periphery. At three feet I can see the world; the countries and their location on the map. From three feet I have a pretty good perspective of the geo-political situation; how countries relate to one another. At six feet I can not only see the world, but I begin to see the mapmaker's plan. The longitudinal and latitudinal lines growing outward as they travel away from the equator are called *"Mercator's Projection."* Without this mapmaker's trick, used since the 16th century, navigators would be unable to plot their course. From six feet I can easily see *"Mercator's Projection"* and other tools the mapmaker included to prevent navigators from becoming lost in the world's oceans.

The lesson of the map is a lesson in perspective – how we see things. Men can only view objects and circumstances from where they are. Viewed from ground level the world is a blur. At ground level, if anything beyond our noses does exist it's out of focus; our life is consumed with the daily struggle of personal existence. Distance, in time and circumstance, brings us greater perspective. Once our immediate survival needs are satisfied, we can step back for a moment and see our situation from a little larger perspective. Time also adds to our perspective. We have the luxury of looking back over our history, learning from mistakes of the past and vowing not to repeat them. The problem remains, however, that our perspective of the world is limited by our relative proximity to it, both in time and space. If we could somehow figuratively escape earth's orbit and the restrictions of time and space, perhaps then we could get the big picture; a real and true perspective of the world and our situation in it; perhaps even some cosmic mapmaker's purpose behind the whole thing.

The good news is that there is a map of our human situation and there is a mapmaker who can guide us as we navigate on life's oceans. God is the Mapmaker. His Word is a map and within its pages are the mapmaker's tools, laid into the map so that we can gain a true perspective of the world and our situation in it. The stories of Abraham, Ishmael, Isaac, Jacob, Esau and Joseph are part of the map of human existence. From those stories the reader gains perspective, not just of the map in general, but of his own relative position in the world. This map is as relevant to the modern navigator as it was to those ancient sojourners whose lives became a part of the map, a part of the story. The

Mapmaker has inserted tools into the map so that we could see the situation in its proper perspective. The Mapmaker's purpose in its creation was to guide men on their life journeys.

God's perspective isn't man's perspective. God's perspective is from above. He's free from time and space. He sees the whole map. He's the Mapmaker. He sees where it begins and where it ends. God's interaction with Abraham, Sarah, Hagar, Ishmael and Isaac, came from a perspective that took into account circumstances that occurred millions of years before they were born and circumstances yet to occur, thousands of years after their deaths. When He spoke to Rebekah as her two sons fought inside her womb, he knew the chain of events that led to their birth and the chain of events that would result from their birth. Today, in the midst of Middle East conflict and the world's trepidation over future oil supply, God sees events, whether they occurred in the 16th century BC or the 21st century AD, from a perspective above that of man.

God's Purpose

God's perspective is tied to His purpose; and God is purposeful. The universe was created on purpose and for God's purpose. This world and the race of men who inhabit it were created on purpose and as a part of God's purpose. When and how this world and its race of men reach the expiration of the current age and begin the next will be according to God's purpose. God doesn't purpose man toward hate and killing and mutual destruction; but in the midst of the hate and killing and destruction, God's purpose remains. In His sovereignty, God chose Isaac and not Ishmael. He preferred Jacob to Esau. In his sovereign purpose, God named the children of Israel as His chosen people and gave them an inheritance in the land of Canaan. This land and all of its resources, above and below the ground, was given by God to Israel and his children as an *"everlasting possession"*.

> Then Jacob (Israel) said to Joseph, God Almighty appeared to me at Luz in the land of Canaan and blessed me, and He said to me, "Behold, I will make you fruitful and numerous, and I will make you a company of peoples, and will give this land to your descendents after you for an everlasting possession.
>
> (Genesis 48:3 NASB)

Prophecy Fulfilled

Is the discovery of a vast oil reserve in the land of Israel really a fulfillment of end time prophecy? Jacob's blessing appears twice in the Old Testament, first from Jacob himself in the 49th chapter of Genesis; then it is repeated in Deuteronomy 33 by Moses 400 years later, to the descendents of Jacob just before they enter the Promised Land. Jacob's blessing is the source of our clues regarding God's promise of oil in Israel. As a preamble to his blessing in Genesis, Jacob tells his sons, *"...Gather yourselves together that I may tell you that which shall befall you in the last days."* (49:1) The blessing described in Genesis 49 was meant for the descendents of Jacob's sons, not the sons themselves. It is a promise to his sons, not for the day it was given, but for the last days.

Does the passage in Deuteronomy in anyway refer to the *"last days"* or should we view the blessing Moses gives to the children of Israel only in the context of that period in history? Moses doesn't say in Deuteronomy, *"Gather yourselves together so that I may tell you that which shall befall you in the last days."* But surely we are not so dull that we need anything as obvious to point us toward the same conclusion. Firstly, this is a repeat of Jacob's original blessing. Moses is restating Jacob's blessing to the descendents of Jacob's twelve sons. If Jacob meant his blessing for the last days when he first gave it to his sons, then Moses could have only meant the same when he restated the blessing to their descendents. If that logic isn't enough there are some other clues in Deuteronomy.

Deuteronomy 32 is called *"The Song of Moses"*. It is his preamble to repeating Jacob's blessing the last time he addresses the Children of Israel. Verses eight and nine speak of a time long before their gathering on the borders of the Promised Land.

> *When the Most High gave the nations their inheritance, When He separated the sons of man, He set the boundaries of the peoples According to the number of the sons of Israel... For the Lord's portion is his people; Jacob is the allotment of His inheritance.*
>
> (NASB)

Remember what we said about perspective? God's perspective sees way before and way ahead. This passage refers to some time early, early on in earth's history. When Moses spoke of God *"giving the nations their inheritance"*, *"separating the sons of man"* and *"setting the boundaries of the people"* he was not speaking in the context of their current age. At the very least this passage reveals that the context refers to a time in the remote past. But let's go on; we've only seen a passage referring to the *"first days"*, we haven't found anything yet referring to the *"last days"*.

Deuteronomy 33 contains Jacob's Blessing given by Moses to the Children of Israel before entering the Promised Land. Verse 17 gives us the clue we are looking for. Speaking of Joseph, Moses prophecies:

> *In majesty he is like a firstborn bull; his horns are the horns of a wild ox. With them he will gore the nations, even those at the ends of the earth.*
>
> (NIV)

Joseph, upon whose head the blessing (oil) rests will be as a bull, whose horns will *"gore the nations, even those at the ends of the earth."* We know Moses couldn't have been speaking in the context of the day. The *"nations at the ends of the earth"* were way outside of the scope of the Israelite's conquest of Canaan. We also know that Joseph *"goring the nations"* isn't an event that has happened to date in recorded history. This passage refers to something that is yet to take place. Isn't it interesting that the Bible reveals that Jacob's blessing (oil) rests on the crown of the head of Joseph and Moses prophesies that the nations will be *"gored"* by the crown of the head of Joseph!

The End of Days

Biblical prophecy is fulfilled for God's purpose, but it is often man's purpose and history's circumstance that precipitates it. Some circumstance in the *"real"* world comes about in order for man to act in accordance with his purpose, in order to set the scene for God's purpose.

A good illustration of man acting according to his own purposes in order to set the scene for God's divine purpose is the Old Testament story of the Pharaoh refusing to release the Children of Israel from Egypt. God's purpose was that the Children of Israel should leave their captivity in Egypt and move into the Promised Land of Canaan. If the Pharaoh had listened to God's spokesman, Moses, when he first requested that the Children of Israel be released, God's purpose (seemingly) would have been fulfilled. *"The Children of Israel leave Egypt, they move to Canaan – God's purpose fulfilled - done deal!"* But that wasn't God's full purpose. God's purpose was to prove, beyond a shadow of a doubt, that He was divine and He was in charge.

Before Moses traveled to Egypt for his meeting with the Pharaoh God showed him some parlor tricks to prove to Pharaoh that Moses spoke for someone greater than himself. God gave Moses the power to turn his walking stick into a serpent and then back to a walking stick again. Moses was given the power to put his hand into his cloak and bring it out leprous; then put it in again and pull it out disease free. Moses was also given the power to turn water into blood. God knew that these magic tricks wouldn't be sufficient to convince Pharaoh to release his population of Jewish slaves, but they proved to Moses that God's power was sufficient to His promise.

While he was still in Midian, God instructed Moses:

"Then say to Pharaoh, 'This is what the Lord says: Israel is my son, my firstborn son, and I told you, "Let my son go, so he may Worship me." But you refused to let him go; so I will kill your firstborn son.'"

(Exodus 4:22-23)

God's words to Moses foreshadowed what would take place before Pharaoh would finally relent and free the Children of Israel. Ten plagues were visited on the people of Egypt, Pharaoh repented continually and continually reneged on his promises. Finally, as a result of the tenth plague, the death of every first born male of Egypt, including Pharaoh's own son, he agreed to release the Children of Israel from their slavery. The Egyptians were so defeated by the plagues and relieved at the Israelites departure that they loaded them with all the wealth of Egypt as they departed.

After a few days with the Children of Israel out of town the Pharaoh began thinking. The slave labor that enabled the economy of Egypt was provided compliments of the Children of Israel. The Egyptian economy would quickly disintegrate without the free labor provided by Jacob's descendents. Whatever it cost the Egyptians needed those slaves back! Pharaoh mounted his army in full pursuit to overtake and capture his former workforce and return them to Egypt. God again miraculously delivered the Children of Israel by opening a dry path in the Red Sea providing the Children of Israel an avenue of escape from the armies of

Pharaoh, then closing it again drowning Pharaoh and his pursuing armies.

When I was in seventh grade, my parochial school instructor related the story of Israel's escape from Pharaoh through the Red Sea. The Red Sea, he told us, was really the *"Sea of Reeds"*, a shallow eighteen inch deep backwater that the Children of Israel could easily wade through to the other side. I was shattered. My entire life in Sunday School I had heard the story of how God had parted the Red Sea and how the Children of Israel had crossed on dry land. Then, as Pharaoh's army entered one end of God's newly formed *"land bridge"* as the last of Israel's people exited the other end, God released the waters and Pharaoh's army was drowned in the resulting torrent. I knew the story, I had seen the pictures displayed on the *"flannel graph"* board in my Sunday School room; now my teacher had broken the magnificent picture in my mind by telling me that the Children of Israel had simply waded across the *"Sea of Reeds"*. I returned home that evening with my head hanging. At supper I related the incident to my father, in whose churches I had learned the original story. He smiled and put his hand on my shoulder, *"That's great news Stevie"*, he said. *"It's a bigger miracle than I thought!"* When my eyes questioned him he explained, *"What a miracle that Pharaoh's entire army was drowned in eighteen inches of water!"*

Pharaoh's army, of course, wasn't drowned in eighteen inches of water, and God did part the Red Sea miraculously; enabling the Children of Israel's escape and Pharaoh's destruction. The point is that God purposed Pharaoh to act in his own interest. God hardened Pharaoh's heart against Moses and the Children of Israel in order that by Pharaoh's actions in his own interest and seemingly for his own purpose, God's divine power and will would be revealed for God's glory. Romans 9:17–18 summarizes God's purpose in Pharaoh actions:

For the Scripture says to Pharaoh: "I raised you up for this very purpose, that I might display my power in you and that my name might be proclaimed in all the earth." Therefore God has mercy on whom he wants to have mercy, and he hardens whom he wants to harden.

(NIV)

Gog and Magog

We learned in Chapter Eight that Russia (Gog and Magog) would be drawn down into Israel to take a *"spoil".* As it was for Pharaoh in the days of Moses, so shall it be for Gog and Magog in the last days. The prophetic Old Testament book of Ezekiel predicts that Gog and Magog (ancient names for what is now Russia) along with Persia (Iran), Ethiopia, Libya, Gomer (Germany?), and Togarmah (Turkey) will be drawn down into Israel. Most of the southern Russian Republics are Islamic. Iran, Ethiopia, Libya, and Turkey are Islamic nations. We can assume that the balance of Arab/Islamic world, with their long standing enmity toward Israel, will join in the fray.

After many days you will be called to arms. In future years you will invade a land that has recovered from war, whose people were gathered from many nations to the mountains of Israel, which had long been desolate. They had been brought out from the nations, and now all of them live in safety. You and all your troops and the many nations with you will go up, advancing like a storm; you will be like a cloud covering the land.

This is what the Sovereign LORD says: "On that day thoughts will come into your mind and you will devise an evil scheme. You will

say, 'I will invade a land of unwalled villages;
I will attack a peaceful and unsuspecting
people—all of them living without walls and
without gates and bars. I will plunder and
loot and turn my hand against the resettled
ruins and the people gathered from the
nations, rich in livestock and goods, living at
the center of the land.'"

(Ezekiel Chapter 38: 8-12 NIV)

These countries will invade a land that is at peace and living in safety. They will have *"devised an evil scheme"* to plunder the Nation of Israel. Russia and her allies will invade Israel for their own purposes, to plunder the land; but, like Pharaoh, it is God's purpose that will direct the action. Earlier in Chapter 38 of Ezekiel, God states:

...I am against you, O Gog...I will turn you
around, put hooks in your jaws and bring you
out with your whole army...

(Vs.3 – 4 NIV)

God orchestrates even the evil intentions of man to His purpose. Like Pharaoh, God's purpose for Gog and his allies is to reveal Himself to the nations.

In the days to come, O Gog, I will bring you
against my land, so that the nations may know
me when I show myself holy through you
before their eyes.

(Ezekiel 38:16 NIV)

What happens when Gog and his allies invade Israel? Just like the pursuing armies of Pharaoh, they will be miraculously destroyed.

I will turn you around and drag you along. I
will bring you from the far north and send you
against the mountains of Israel. Then I will
strike your bow from your left hand and make
your arrows drop from your right hand. On
the mountains of Israel you will fall, you and

> *all your troops and the nations with you. I
> will give you as food to all kinds of carrion
> birds and to the wild animals. You will fall in
> the open field, for I have spoken, declares the
> Sovereign LORD. I will send fire on Magog
> and on those who live in safety in the
> coastlands, and they will know that I am the
> LORD.*
>
> (Ezekiel 38: 2-6 NIV)

The End Game

What is God's final purpose? What's the end game?
Why would He pit nation against nation? What possible
reason could He have for promising Jacob's sons a vast oil
reserve, only to be discovered in the last days? Why involve
Russia?

God's final purpose is his first purpose. His
beginning game is the same as His end game.

> *And so I will show my greatness and my
> holiness, and I will make myself known in the
> sight of many nations. Then they will know
> that I am the Lord.*
>
> (Ezekiel 38:23)

> *I will make known my holy name among my
> people Israel. I will no longer let my holy
> name be profaned, and the nations will know
> that I the LORD am the Holy One in Israel.*
>
> (Ezekiel 39:7 NIV)

What about the nation of Israel? Does God have a
purpose for the people of modern day Israel? Will they be
destroyed by their own blessing? Will Russia and her allies
invade Israel to destroy her and take her oil in the last days?

Ezekiel 39 tells us that just the opposite will happen.
God will destroy the armies of Gog and Magog and not only
will Israel be saved, they will be redeemed. Don't lose sight -

God's final purpose is his original purpose. His beginning game is the same as His end game. His purpose from the beginning was and is to reveal Himself first and foremost to His chosen people Israel, then to the nations.

From that day forward the house of Israel will know that I am the LORD their God. And the nations will know that the people of Israel went into exile for their sin, because they were unfaithful to me. So I hid my face from them and handed them over to their enemies, and they all fell by the sword. I dealt with them according to their uncleanness and their offenses, and I hid my face from them.

"Therefore this is what the Sovereign LORD says: I will now bring Jacob back from captivity and will have compassion on all the people of Israel, and I will be zealous for my holy name. They will forget their shame and all the unfaithfulness they showed toward me when they lived in safety in their land with no one to make them afraid. When I have brought them back from the nations and have gathered them from the countries of their enemies, I will show myself holy through them in the sight of many nations. Then they will know that I am the LORD their God, for though I sent them into exile among the nations, I will gather them to their own land, not leaving any behind. I will no longer hide my face from them, for I will pour out my Spirit on the house of Israel, declares the Sovereign LORD."

(Ezekiel 39:22-29)

APPENDICES

SPIRITUAL HELP

Are you looking for answers? Here you will find direction and encouragement for your pursuit of the Way, the Truth, and the Life.

How to Become a Christian

The central theme of the Bible is God's love for you and for all people. This love was revealed when Jesus Christ, the Son of God, came into the world as a human being, lived a sinless life, died on the cross, and rose from the dead. Because Christ died, your sins can be forgiven, and because He conquered death you can have eternal life. You can know for sure what will become of you after you die.

You have probably heard the story of God's love referred to as the "Gospel." The word Gospel simply means "Good News." The Gospel is the Good News that, because of what Christ has done, we can be forgiven and can live forever.

But this gift of forgiveness and eternal life cannot be yours unless you willingly accept it. God requires an individual response from you. The following verses from the Bible show God's part and yours in this process:

God's Love Is Revealed in the Bible
"For God so loved the world that he gave his one and only Son, that whoever believes in him shall not perish but have eternal life." — John 3:16 (NIV)

God loves you. He wants to bless your life and make it full and complete. And He wants to give you a life which will last forever, even after you experience physical death.

We Are Sinful

"For all have sinned and fall short of the glory of God." —Romans 3:23 (NIV)

You may have heard someone say, "I'm only human—nobody's perfect." This Bible verse says the same thing: We are all sinners. We all do things that we know are wrong. And that's why we feel estranged from God—because God is holy and good, and we are not.

Sin Has a Penalty
"For the wages of sin is death." —Romans 6:23 (NIV)

Just as criminals must pay the penalty for their crimes, sinners must pay the penalty for their sins. If you continue to sin, you will pay the penalty of spiritual death: You will not only die physically; you will also be separated from our holy God for all eternity. The Bible teaches that those who choose to remain separated from God will spend eternity in a place called hell.

Christ Has Paid Our Penalty!
"But God demonstrates his own love for us in this: While we were still sinners, Christ died for us." —Romans 5:8 (NIV)

The Bible teaches that Jesus Christ, the sinless Son of God, has paid the penalty for all your sins. You may think you have to lead a good life and do good deeds before God will love you. But the Bible says that Christ loved you enough to die for you, even when you were rebelling against Him.

Salvation Is a Free Gift
"For it is by grace you have been saved, through faith—and this not from yourselves, it is the gift of God—not by works, so that no one can boast." —Ephesians 2:8-9 (NIV)

The word grace means "undeserved favor." It means God is offering you something you could never provide for yourself: forgiveness of sins and eternal life, God's gift to you is free. You do not have to work for a gift. All you have to do is joyfully receive it, Believe with all your heart that Jesus Christ died for you!

Christ Is at Your Heart's Door

Here I am! I stand at the door and knock. If anyone hears my voice and opens the door, I will come in and eat with him, and he with me." —Revelation 3:20 (NIV)

Jesus Christ wants to have a personal relationship with you. Picture, if you will, Jesus Christ standing at the door of your heart (the door of your emotions, intellect and will). Invite Him in; He is waiting for you to receive Him into your heart and life.

You Must Receive Him

"Yet to all who received him, to those who believed in his name, he gave the right to become children of God." —John 1:12 (NIV)

When you receive Christ into your heart you become a child of God, and have the privilege of talking to Him in prayer at any time about anything. The Christian life is a personal relationship to God through Jesus Christ. And best of all, it is a relationship that will last for all eternity.

APPENDIX B
ZION OIL & GAS VISION BOOK

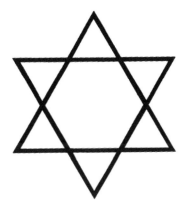

THE OIL OF IS'RA-EL

"Write the vision; make it plain upon tablets, so he may run who reads it. For still the vision awaits its time; it hastens to end - it will not lie. If it seems slow, wait for it; it will surely come, it will not delay"

– Habakkuk 2: 2&3

FOUNDER'S TESTIMONY

THE VISION AND THE CALLING

Dear Friends,

When first visiting Israel in 1983, I believe G-d gave me a scripture (I Kings 8:41-43), a vision (Oil for Israel) and, as a Christian Zionist and New Covenant believer (Isaiah 65:1), the calling to render assistance to the Jewish people and Nation of Israel and to aid them in the Restoration of the Land by providing the oil and gas necessary to help the People of Israel maintain their political and economic independence. (Leviticus 19:33, 34) (Exodus 6:6-8)

In the Bible, G-d sovereignty declares that Israel is His chosen people (Exodus 4:22); and we can gain some understanding of G-d's choice, His vision and purpose by reading (Deuteronomy 7).

As a Christian Zionist, I declare "thy people shall be my people, and thy God my God" (Ruth 1:16); and, I believe that, as true Christians, we must all so identify with Israel, as we are all part of the "wild olive branch" grafted onto the olive tree by the grace of G-d (Romans 11). Moreover, I identify with Israel because I share in their struggle and understand a little something of their pain, their confusion, their hope, the media misrepresentation, and the world's disdain of the Jewish people and the nation of Israel even and perhaps more so today, when Israel appears to be coming under greater criticism for raking those very steps of self-defense which we in America take for granted as our sovereign moral right to take in defense of ourselves and our interests.

As a believer, I have and can have no doubt that mankind must learn that obedience towards G-d and His commandments is the key to progress, whether personal or corporate, national or international. Disobedience, on the other hand, can lead only to great difficulty. This too is the story of the Jewish people and the nation of Israel. And, indeed it appears that G-d's chosen people have ascended to heights and descended to depths far beyond our experience - in both blessings and curses - in progress and disaster.

In considering the history of Israel, however, this principle alone is insufficient to explain the great magnitude of Israel's sufferings. There is another dimension. Through the centuries, the millennia, Israel has been and continues to be a tangible and visible target for dark spiritual forces which are directed against the living G-d himself. No one can touch G-d; but the individual Jew and the nation of Israel are within reach of those whose hatred is directed against G-d, and who would foil the fulfillment of His purposes and disrupt His plan for the people of His covenant and the nation of Israel.

This hatred has been manifested time and again throughout the ages. To name only a sampling, there have been the crusades, the inquisition, the pogroms. In this century, we have seen the Holocaust, as well as the humiliation of and later reneging on, numerous agreements regarding the land of promise. Since the re-establishment of the State of Israel in 1948, there have been many wars and many more terrorist attacks. Most recently, there has been the Gulf War with scud missiles, threatening chemical mayhem. Then there was, and continues to be, the forced pressure of the 'peace' negotiations and calls of "land for peace" despite the fact that Israel is the only nation on Earth that was created by a sovereign act of G-d (Genesis 15) and whose borders are defined by G-d (Numbers 34:1-12). For in (Exodus 32: 13) He said, "...All of this land which I have spoken of will I give to your descendants and they shall inherit it **forever**."

And when in the summer of the year 2000, the Prime Minister of Israel indicated that in return for the much prayed for peace Israel would be willing to give most all of the territory of the Holy Land re-conquered in the 1967 War - a war commenced by the Arabs with the declared purpose of destroying Israel - to the Palestinians for them to be a state, those very Palestinians rejected the offer, declaring that the Jews had no right to Jerusalem or to the Temple Mount, that the Bible was "forged" to show such a connection between the people of Israel and the site of His House, and then commenced a wave of terrorism, sending human bombs to kill and maim teenagers at discotheques and families at pizza lunches.

Yet the recent events in the land of Israel notwithstanding, with sorrow and regret, we must admit the truth and confess that the greatest sufferings imposed on the Jewish people and Israel throughout history have come from the so-called Christian church and from those confessing the Christian faith. <u>For this we must all ask their forgiveness</u>. The forces directed against the Jews have misrepresented G-d and have wrongly interpreted His Word in an attempt to rob Israel of its inheritance which is based on (Genesis 17:7-8) a sovereign promise from G-d (Exodus 6:4) and an everlasting covenant (Deuteronomy 4:31). Despite the fact that these expressions of evil are totally contrary to G-d's everlasting covenant, His unchanging nature and purpose, these actions were and continue to be "justified" by these evil men and nations for their own ends.

But as the Bible declares, G-d HAS NOT forsaken His covenant people (Jeremiah 31:31-40); and, "as new covenant believers, we are commanded by G-d in the Bible to stand together with the Jewish people whom the world has abused, As the fulfillment of prophecy is for the Jewish people - for them the realization of their covenant and for them the answer to their prayers of countless generations:

"And I will plant them upon their land, and they shall no more be pulled up out of their land which I have given them, saith the Lord thy God."   (Amos 9:14-15).

John Brown

Founder (Amos 3:7)

THE SCRIPTURES GIVEN TO JOHN BROWN

THE QUESTION AND THE ANSWER...The Blessings of the Fathers (*Genesis Chapters 17, 27, 49 and Deuteronomy Chapters 32,33*)

The economic and political stability of Israel, indeed, its very survival is at stake not in any small measure because of its dependence on imported oil and gas. The desire to free Israel of such dependence has opened up unexplored areas of Israel and, today, more sophisticated exploitation and drilling techniques than previously used are being utilized to assess the oil potential of those areas.

The State of Israel lies in the heart of the Middle East and is surrounded by areas in neighboring Arab countries which contain the world's largest oil fields. These oil fields are the blessings and posterity which G-d had promised Abraham also for his son Ishmael in (Genesis 17:18-20) and by Isaac's blessing also of his son Esau in (Genesis 27:38-39). The genealogies of Ishmael (Genesis 25:12-18) and Esau (Genesis 36) show that their descendants became the inhabitants of modern day Saudi Arabia -and other Arab countries from Egypt to Iraq, Jordan to Yemen.

The State of Israel, as a member of the free world and as the only true, stable democracy in the Middle East, strives to find oil to remain independent from outside political pressures.

In 1988, the Government of Israel, acting through the government-owned Oil Exploration Investments Ltd., its affiliates and subsidiaries and geological consultants of renowned international reputation, established the hydrocarbon potential of Israel, and validated the existence of significant quantities of recoverable oil and gas in the Land of Israel, as also exist in the neighboring countries of the Middle East.

Past exploration efforts have yielded several small on-shore discoveries and the recent, significant gas fields off-shore in the Mediterranean Sea. But the "real potential" still awaits discovery!

Following continued assessment of all geological and geophysical data, renowned petroleum engineers, geologists and geophysicists continue to ask ... "where is the most logical place to drill where we can be sure of 'tapping' those vast reservoirs of oil?"

Yet, there is an "ANSWER", and **it** is found in the most "overlooked" source of geological information available to mankind today the Bible! The archaeologists have found the Bible to be their unerring guide to hidden treasures ... Why cannot the geologists utilize the same "tool" to find this oil?

So we searched the Bible and found numerous occasions where, I believe, the Bible in describing the division of the Land of Israel among the sons of Jacob - commencing in Genesis (Chapter 49) when Jacob on his deathbed summons his sons and says *"Gather yourselves together, that I might tell you that which shall befall you in the LAST DAYS"* (Genesis 49:1) and concluding in Deuteronomy (Chapters 32 and 33) with Moses' song of praise of G-d and his blessings of the twelve tribes as G-d prepares him to view the "Promised Land" which HE had given to HIS chosen

"Children of Israel" - makes direct reference to the existence of OIL in Israel.

So, friends of Israel, as we begin "The Great Treasure Hunt" ... may we join hands with the Government of Israel and its people and together look toward and pray for "the discovery of OIL in their homeland, the Land of Israel" and on the "Head of Joseph" as promised in the Torah by the G-d of Abraham, Isaac and Jacob (Genesis 49:25, 26) (Deuteronomy 33:13-16); and then G-d said, *"I will even gather you from the peoples, and assemble you out of the countries where ye have been scattered, and I will give you the land of Israel"* (Ezekiel 11:17) and Israel will be graciously comforted and restored. (Micah 7:18-20), (Ezekiel 37:15-28)

THE VISION ... The Oil Of Is'ra-el

While visiting Israel with Alger Wolfe in May 1983, John Brown's prayer to the G-d of Abraham, Isaac and Jacob was for oil to be found in Israel. This prayer and G-d's specific instruction to John were based on the Biblical portion describing the Dedication of the First Temple in Jerusalem and Solomon's prayers thereat. (I Kings 8:22-66)

ONE ... The Prayer

"Moreover concerning a stranger [John Brown], *that is not of thy people Israel but cometh out of a far country* [U.S.A.] *for thy name's sake: (for they shall hear of thy great name, and of thy strong hand and of thy stretched out arm); when he shall come and pray towards this house; hear thou in heaven thy dwelling place, and do according to ALL that the*

stranger calleth to thee for [Oil for Israel]: *that all the people of the earth may know thy name, to fear thee, as do thy people Israel and that thy may know that this house, which I have builded, is called by thy name. '(1 Kings 8:41-43).*

TWO ... The Instructions

"And it shall come to pass, if ye shall hearken diligently unto my commandments which I command you this day, to love the Lord your God and to serve Him with all your heart and with all your soul, that I will give you the rain of your land in his due season, the early rain and the late rain, that thou mayest gather in thy corn, and thy wine, and thine OIL [the OIL of Israel]." *(Deuteronomy 11:13-14)*

THREE ... The Evidence

"Then thou shalt see, and flow together, and thine heart shall fear, and be enlarged- because the abundance of the sea shall be converted unto thee, the forces of the Gentiles shall come unto thee." (Isaiah 60:5)

These three specific sets of instructions received by John Brown in 1983 from G-d while in the land of Israel, were a consuming "fire" which has been born by him through the years for the exact purpose that G-d first lit it in his heart! Today, G-d continues to confirm, by HIS Word, the reality of HIS promise when HE also promised...

"For surely there is an end and thy expectation shall not be cut off" (Proverbs 23:18)

THE CALLING... Tell Them...

So, then He told me to *"write the vision"* (Habakkuk 2:2, 3) and tell them:

"And the word of the Lord came unto me, saying, 'Son of man, what is that proverb that ye have in the land of Israel, saying, The days are prolonged, and every vision faileth? Tell them therefore, Thus saith the Lord God; I will make this proverb to cease, and they shall no more use it as a proverb in Israel but say unto them, The days are at hand, and the effect of every vision. For there shall be no more any vain vision nor flattering divination within the house of Israel. For I am the Lord: I will speak, and the word that I shall speak shall come to pass; it shall be no more prolonged: for in your days, 0 rebellious house, will l say the word, and will perform it, saith the Lord God"

"Again the word of the Lord came to me saying, 'Son of man, behold they of the house of Israel say, The vision that he seeth is for many days to come, and he prophesieth of the times that are far off. Therefore say unto them, Thus saith the Lord God; There shall none of my words be prolonged any more, but the word which I have spoken shall be done, saith the Lord God'" (Ezekiel 12: 21-28)

THE PROMISES...Also Unto the Gentiles *(Leviticus 19:33, 34)*

For the prophets foretold that Gentiles (Isaiah 55:5) would also call upon G-d and they too would serve him (Zephaniah 3:9) and he would answer their prayers (Isaiah 65:24) and he would save them (Isaiah 52:10) and set them in the land! (Isaiah 14:1) For it is also written:

"Also the sons of the stranger, that join themselves to the Lord, to serve Him, and to love the name of the Lord, to be His servants, every one that keepeth the Sabbath and does not profane it, and all that hold fast to my covenant. Even them will I bring to my holy mountain, and make them joyful in my house of prayer; their burnt offerings and their sacrifices shall be accepted on my altar: for my house shall be called a house of prayer for all peoples.' (Isaiah 56: 6-7)

A NEW COVENANT PEOPLE ... *Jeremiah 31: 31-34)*

For G-d has promised that not only would He honor his First Covenant and would cause the Jews to return (Jeremiah 33:14-26), but that one day He would also make a New Covenant (Jeremiah 31:33-34) and (in Hosea 2:23) He said: *"...And I will say to them that were not my people; Thou art my people!"* And they shall say, *"you are my God"* and they will help restore the Nation of Israel and many people would come to the Land of Israel to seek the G-d of Israel (Zechariah 8:20-23) (Isaiah 65:1) and these strangers who dwelt among the people of Israel would also share in the promised inheritance (Ezekiel 47:21-23) and... *"the stranger that dwells with you shall be to you as one born among you."* (Leviticus 19:34) For G-d's promise to Abraham was, *"and in thy seed shall **all the nations of the earth be blessed.**"* (Genesis 22:18)

So now we, a new covenant people, (Deuteronomy 29:12-15) have come to the land of Israel to claim our promised inheritance and to receive the blessings of Abraham (Galatians 3:6-14). For it is also written, *"...is He the God of the Jews only? Is HE not the God of the Gentiles? Yes, of the Gentiles also"* (Romans 3:29-30) for G-d hath not cast away HIS people which HE foreknew. *"For if their* [the Jewish people] *being cast away is the reconciling of the world, what will their acceptance be but life from the dead?"* (Romans 11:1-24). Because, *"that blindness in part has happened to Israel until the fullness of the Gentiles be come in. And <u>so all Israel will be saved.</u>"* (Romans 11:24-36) Therefore:

As a Christian, one must recognize that it is written "*... if* [we] *the Gentiles have been made partakers of their* [Israel's] *spiritual things, their* [Gentiles'] *duty is also to minister to them* [Israel] *in material things."* (Romans 15:27) Because *"the G-d of heaven He will prosper us* [Zion]" (Nehemiah 2:20) with the oil of Israel ... so that we a new covenant people of Zion will minister and assist "Israel in their petroleum and material needs." Because, as touching the election, *"they* [the Jewish People] *are beloved for the sake of the fathers."* (Romans 11:28) And, when they do turn to the Lord, the veil on their hearts will be taken away. (2 Corinthians 3:14-16)

THE PURPOSE...

To Receive The Blessings Of Jacob *(Genesis 49:1-2 and 22-26)*

Zion Oil & Gas was ordained by G-d for the express purpose of discovering oil and gas in the Land of Israel and to bless the Jewish people and the nation of Israel and the body of Christ. (Isaiah 23:18) I believe that G-d has promised in the Bible to bless Israel with one of the world's largest oil and gas fields and this will be discovered in the last days before the Messiah returns and that it will be found on the Ma'anit License and the Joseph Permit, both being on the Head of Joseph (Genesis 49:1-2 and 22-26):

"And Jacob called unto his Sons, and said, Gather yourselves together, that I may tell you that which shall befall you in the last days. Gather yourselves together, and hear, ye sons of Jacob; and listen unto Israel your Father ... Joseph is a fruitful bough, a fruitful bough by a well; whose branches run over the wall. The archers fiercely attacked him and shot at him and hated him; but his bow abode in strength, and the arms of his hands were made supple by the hands of the mighty God of Jacob (by the name of shepherd, the Rock of Israel), by the God of thy father who shall help thee; and by the Almighty who shall bless thee, with blessings of the heaven above, blessings of the deep [the Oil of Israel] *that couches beneath; blessings of the breasts and the womb. The blessings of thy Father are mighty beyond the blessings of the eternal mountains, the blessings of the everlasting hills* [Oil], *they shall be on the head of Joseph, and on the crown of the head of him that was separated from his brothers."*

...And The Blessing Of Moses *(Deuteronomy 33:1,13-19)*

"And this is the blessing which Moses the man of GOD blessed the sons of Israel before his death." (Deuteronomy 33:1)

"...And of Joseph he said, blessed of the Lord be his land, for the precious things of heaven, for the dew and for the deep [the Oil of Israel] *that coucheth beneath, and for the precious fruits brought forth by the sun, and for the precious things put forth by the moon, and for the chief things of the ancient mountains and for the precious things of primordial hills* [Oil] *and fullness thereof and for the Good will of HIM that dwelt in the bush; let the blessing* [the Oil of Israel] *come upon the head of Joseph, and upon the top of the head*

of him that was separated from his brethren;" (Deuteronomy 33:13-16);

"They shall call the peoples to the mountain; there they shall offer sacrifices of righteousness; for they shall suck of the abundance of the seas, and of treasures [the Oil of Israel] *hid in the sand "(Deuteronomy 33:19,)*

THE JOSEPH PROJECT

...The Inheritance *(Genesis 48:1 5-22)*

"Joseph shall have two portions. And you shall inherit it, one as well as another; that concerning which I lifted up my hand to give it to your fathers; and this land shall fall to you as an inheritance." (Ezekiel 47:13-14)

"And it shall come to pass, that you shall divide it by lot for an inheritance to you, and to the strangers [Gentile believers] *that sojourn among you, who shall beget children among you: and they shall be to you as those born in the country among the children of Israel; they shall have an inheritance with you among the tribes of Israel. And it shall come to pass, that in whatever tribe the stranger may stay there you shall give him his inheritance, says the Lord GOD." (Ezekiel 4 7:22-23)*

...The Plan ...By Faith *(Hebrews 11:1-40)*

Zion's approach is somewhat unprecedented ...and that is because of its founder's, John Brown's, FAITH in G-d and HIS promises (Joshua 1:8) and in G-d's faithfulness and ability to perform all HIS Word, as we also walk in the steps of faith as Our Father Abraham walked. (Romans 4:11-25)

And Jesus said, *"It is written* [Deuteronomy 8:3], *Man shall not live by bread alone, but by every word of God."* (Luke 4:4)

Now, *"FAITH is the substance of things* [the Oil of Israel] *hoped for, the evidence of things not seen....* [And, it is also written that] *By FAITH Abraham, when he was tested, offered up Isaac, and.. By FAITH Isaac blessed Jacob and Esau concerning things to come; ...By FAITH Jacob, when he was dying, blessed each of the sons of Joseph."* (Hebrews 11:1-22) G-d's word establishes and so states *"... The JUST shall live by his FAITH* (Habakkuk 2:4) *...But without FAITH, it is impossible to please HIM.* "(Hebrews 10:38 and 11:6)

For: We worship by faith as Abel. We walk by faith as Enoch. We work by faith as Noah. We live by faith as Abraham. We govern by faith as Moses. We follow by faith as Israel. We fight by faith as Joshua. We conquer by faith as Gideon. By faith we are patient in suffering, courageous in battle, made strong out of weakness, and are victorious in defeat. We are more than conquerors by our faith seeing *"...there is one God who will justify the circumcised By Faith and the uncircumcised through faith.* "(Romans 3:29-30) So, it is only through faith in JESUS CHRIST that we are saved. *"It is written in the prophets, 'And they shall all be taught by God'* (Isaiah 54:13) *Therefore everyone who hath heard, AND HATH LEARNED OF THE FATHER, cometh unto me."* (John 6:45-51)

From its inception, G-d's plan was born through Faith in G-d's Word into the heart of John Brown, Zion's founder, and, in all matters concerning Zion, the Word of G-d has been the basis of John Brown's conduct and actions: For it is written, *"This book of Law shall not depart from your mouth, but you shall meditate in it day and night, that you may observe to do according to all that is written in it."* (Joshua 1:8) Consequently, the founder of *Zion* shall respect *and "Fear God, and keep HIS commandments: for that is the WHOLE duty of man."* (Ecclesiastes 12:13)

NOW BY FAITH ... The Ma'anit License #298 and the Joseph Permit #176

Preparations are now being made to complete the Ma'anit #1 well in ISRAEL.. For I believe that G-d has promised in the Bible that, in the last days, oil will be discovered in Israel on the head of Joseph. (Genesis 49:1)

... *"by the God of thy father who shall help thee; and by the ALMIGHTY who shall bless thee, with blessings Of HEAVEN above, blessings of the DEEP* [the Oil of Israel] *THAT LIETH BENEATH;...they shall be on the head of Joseph, and on the crown of him that was separated from his brethren"* (Genesis 49:25-26)

... *"And of Joseph he said, blessed of the LORD be his land, for the precious things of HEAVEN, for the dew and for the DEEP* [the Oil of Israel] *THAT COUCHETH BENEATH ...and, for the chief things of the ancient mountains and for the precious things* [Meged] *of the primordial hills* [Oil] *and fullness thereof and for the Good will of Him that dwelt in the bush; let the blessing* [the Oil of Israel] *come upon the head of Joseph, and upon the top of the head of him that was separated from his brethren".* (Deuteronomy 33:13-16) *"And of Asher he said, Be Asher blessed above sons; let him be acceptable to his brethren, and let him **DIP HIS FOOT IN OIL.** "*(Deuteronomy 33:24)

215

Breaking the Treasure Code

(See biblical map on the next page for the location of the Ma'anit License, Joseph Permit and Ma'anit #1 well in relation to the lands of Joseph's children, Ephraim and Manasseh and the lands of Asher.)

RECOMMENDED READING: …

"Breaking the Treasure Code, The Hunt for Israel's Oil" by James R. Spillman & Steven M. Spillman

Order From:

True Potential Publishing

PO Box 904

Travelers Rest, SC 29690 USA

Phone (864) 836-4111   Fax (864) 836-9680

www.oilinisrael.net

"Faith for Earth's Final Hour" by Hal Lindsey

Order From:

Oracle House Publishing

PO Box 1131

Murrietta, CA 92564 USA

Phone: 1-800-TITUS35

www.hallindsey.com

A DVD copy of John Brown's testimony, as aired on TCT Alive on April 21, 2005, can be ordered at no charge via e-mail from jb@zionoil.com or by calling Zion Oil at 214-221-4610.

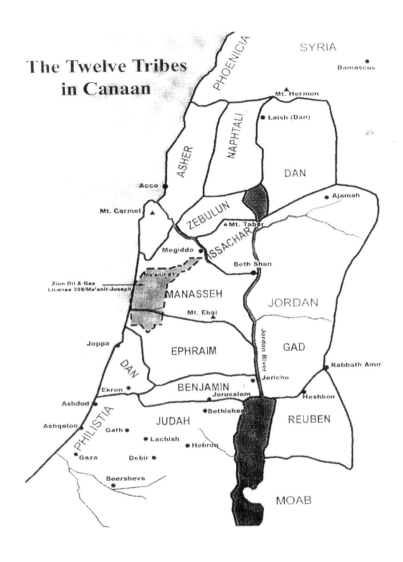

The Twelve Tribes
in Canaan

Other books by
James R. Spillman

- Omega Cometh
- Animal Church
- A Conspiracy of Angels
- The Fire of God
- The Resurrection Clock
- Parables of Light
- The Seven Israels
- Treasures of the Deep

Visit: *www.JimSpillmanMinistries.org* for a full listing of resources available from the works of James R. Spillman

About the Authors

James R. Spillman

Jim Spillman, author, evangelist, and Christian educator was widely known for his charismatic ministry and personality. An ordained Conservative Baptist minister since 1960, Jim served in many churches of varied denominations and backgrounds. As an evangelist and author Jim used his unique mix of spiritual and educational depth with humor to reach people where they were. Audiences around the world were captivated by the power of God demonstrated in his life and brought to Christ for salvation, baptism, healing, and other mighty works of renewal. His background in education allowed him to develop a highly successful teaching style, enabling students to learn great volumes of material of the Word of God in a short length of time.

Jim possessed one of the largest personal libraries in the ministry with many thousands of volumes on the shelves of his converted barn library. The section on eschatology (end-times) alone has several hundred volumes. With undergraduate and graduate degrees in history and Greek, his library specializes in these subjects. Jim used this vast treasure as a resource for his writing.

Jim left this earth for his eternal home in late 2003. His work, however, continues to touch people's lives through books, and recorded material that remain as fresh and relevant today as when they were first produced. Jim's story and resources can be found at www.JimSpillmanMinistries.org.

About the Authors

Steven M. Spillman

Steve Spillman, resides with his wife, Elaine in the foothills of the Blue Ridge Mountains in South Carolina. One of six children of Jim and Nancy Spillman, Steve is an active businessman, owning companies in publishing, manufacturing and real estate. As founder of True Potential Publishing, Inc. he writes and publishes his own work and that of several new and established authors, including his father's previous works. True Potential Publishing's full product offering can be found at www.tppress.com

TRUE POTENTIAL PUBLISHING
QUICK ORDER FORM

 website: go to www.tppress.com

 telephone orders: (864) 836-4111

 fax orders: (864) 836-9680

 email orders: info@tppress.com

 postal orders: True Potential Publishing

PO Box 904, Travelers Rest, SC 29690

___copies of <u>THE TREASURES OF THE DEEP</u> @ $9.95

___copies of <u>BREAKING THE TREASURE CODE, The Hunt for Israel's Oil</u>

@ $14.95

Sales tax: Please add 5% sales tax to items shipped to SC

Shipping by air: US add $4.00 for first book and $2.00 for each additional book.

Name:

_____

Address:

_____

_____

City:_____

Zip:_____

Telephone:_____

e-mail: _____

Payment: ☐ **Check** ☐ **Visa** ☐ **MasterCard**
Card Number:

_____

Name on card: _____

Exp. date:_____